Published by Time-Life Books, London 2001

Time-Life is a trademark of Time Warner Inc., USA

PARENT'S GUIDES TO PLAY

Produced by Weldon Owen Publishing
814 Montgomery Street, San Francisco, California 94133
In collaboration with the Gymboree Corporation, Inc.
700 Airport Boulevard, Burlingame, California 94010

GENERAL EDITOR
Dr. Wendy S. Masi

EDITORIAL CONSULTANTS
Dr. Anthony D. Pellegrini
Dr. Marilyn Segal

GYMBOREE PLAY & MUSIC PROGRAMS
Program & Training Manager: **Kathy Erle**
Senior Program Developer & Trainer: **Helene Silver Freda**
Product Manager: **Julie Fraser**
Creative Manager: **Melissa Benavidez**

Copyright © 2001 The Gym-Mark, Inc.
and Weldon Owen, Inc.

All rights reserved. Unauthorized reproduction,
in any manner, is prohibited.

10 9 8 7 6 5 4 3 2 1

ISBN 0-7054-3405-2

Printed in Singapore.

WELDON OWEN PUBLISHING
Chief Executive Officer: **John Owen**
President: **Terry Newell**
Chief Operating Officer: **Larry Partington**
Vice President, International Sales: **Stuart Laurence**
Vice President & Publisher: **Roger S. Shaw**
Associate Publisher: **Rebecca Poole Forée**
Writers: **Mona Behan, Susan E. Davis,**
Christine Loomis, Genevieve Morgan
Copy Editor: **Mandy Erickson**
Contributing Editors: **Laura Buller, Cynthia Rubin,**
Lisa Zuniga
Proofreader: **Karin Mullen**
Indexer: **Ken DellaPenta**

Art Director: **Emma Forge**
Design Manager: **Brynn Breuner**
Photographer: **Chris Shorten**
Production Director: **Stephanie Sherman**
Production Managers: **Lisa Cowart-Mayor, Chris Hemesath**
Production Assistants: **William Erik Evans,**
Lisa Lee, Joan Olson
Illustrator: **Matt Graif**
Contributing Designer: **Elizabeth Marken**
Photographer's Assistant: **Mona Long**

SPECIAL NOTE ON SAFETY PRECAUTIONS

At Gymboree, we encourage parents to become active play partners with their children. As you enjoy these enriching activities with your toddler, be sure to make safety your priority. While the risk of injury during any of these activities is low, Gymboree encourages you to take every precaution to make sure your child is as safe as possible. To reduce the risk of injury, please follow these guidelines: Do not leave your child unattended, even for a brief moment, during any of the activities in this book; be particularly cautious when participating in the activities involving water because of the risk of drowning; ensure that your child does not place in his or her mouth any small objects (even those depicted in the photos) as some may pose a choking hazard and could be fatal if ingested; make sure crayons, markers, and other writing materials are nontoxic and approved for use by children under three years of age.

Throughout Toddler Play we have suggested guidelines to the age-appropriateness of each activity, but please assess your own toddler's suitability for a particular activity beforehand, as ability, balance, and dexterity vary considerably from child to child.

While we have made every effort to ensure that the information in this book is accurate and reliable and that the suggested activities are safe and workable when an adult is properly supervising, we disclaim all liability for any unintended, unforeseen, or improper application of the recommendations and suggestions featured in Toddler Play.

Toddler play

GYMBOREE PLAY & MUSIC
PARENT'S GUIDE

Toddler Play

General Editor
Dr. Wendy S. Masi

Foreword by
Dr. Anthony D. Pellegrini

TIME
LIFE
BOOKS

CONTENTS

TYPES OF ACTIVITIES

FOREWORD

DR. ANTHONY D. PELLEGRINI

Ever since I began teaching in the 1970s, I have been fascinated by watching toddlers play. What a force of nature they are— so full of energy, resourcefulness, and curiosity. They always approach play with a vigour that suggests it's their life's work, which indeed it is at the ripe old age of one or two: play is a way toddlers learn about the world and prime themselves for future achievements. Watching them inspired me to make it my life's work as well, and I've now spent more than twenty-five years in the field of educational psychology, researching the influence play has on the social, emotional, and cognitive development of young children.

I now know that all play isn't equal. Watching television for hours is too passive an occupation to provide the mental and physical stimulation toddlers need; engaging them in a rigidly prescribed activity that runs counter to their personalities or play styles won't do them much good either. For play to be meaningful, children need social interaction, enthusiasm, variety, and some degree of control. They also need partners who are sensitive to their cues and will provide encouragement and affection. In other words, they need you, their parents.

Just because toddlers naturally turn to their parents—and other caregivers—as play partners doesn't mean that keeping up with these intrepid explorers isn't sometimes a challenge. Just trying to think of activities that will keep them happily busy can tax the resources of the most imaginative person. That's where this book comes in. Drawing upon two decades of experience as America's foremost provider of parent-and-child play programmes, Gymboree has created a valuable tool to inspire creative and productive play sessions in the home and on family trips. The variety of activities respects a child's need for many types of play, and the flexibility of the guidelines encourages parents to tailor the games and projects to suit their toddler's own inclinations and abilities. Above all, the activities conform to Gymboree's philosophy of "play with a purpose": they are designed to foster a wide spectrum of cognitive, social, and physical skills—and they just happen to be a whole lot of fun!

I'm confident that you'll find *Toddler Play* an enriching and inspirational resource, one that you'll turn to again and again.

Dr. Anthony D. Pellegrini
Professor, Educational Psychology
University of Minnesota

PLAY WITH A PURPOSE

WHETHER THEIR expressions are marked by ear-to-ear grins or brow-furrowing intensity, toddlers at play are a wonder to behold. The concentration with which they examine—and whoops! occasionally disassemble—each new object, the enthusiasm they bring to each new endeavour, and the joy they radiate as they acquire each new skill

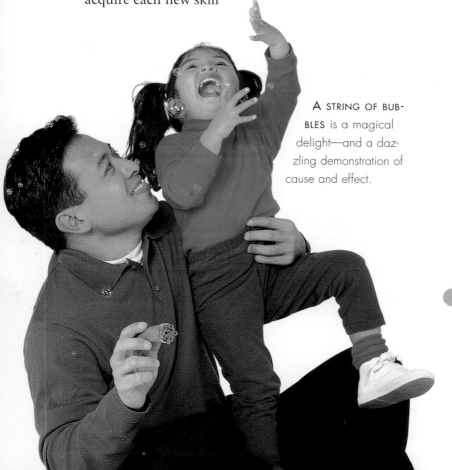

A STRING OF BUB-BLES is a magical delight—and a dazzling demonstration of cause and effect.

demonstrate that for these young explorers, play is serious business. It's a way of learning about their world, other people, and themselves, of testing and pushing the limits of their abilities, of conquering everything from the physics of sand castles to the basic rules of social interaction.

These early years are ripe with unparalleled opportunities for you as a parent to unlock your child's potential. A toddler's brain is a work in progress profoundly influenced by her environment, and what she is now exposed to—or not exposed to—will have a lifelong impact. This might be a daunting prospect except for a few comforting facts. First, children are born primed to learn. Second, parents instinctively strive to provide the stimulation children need. And, most important, since play is a vehicle of learning for children, engaging in this task should be fun for parent and child alike.

THE BENEFITS OF PLAY

Because play comes so naturally to children and seems like nothing more than simple pleasure, it is easy to overlook the many far-reaching benefits that

COORDINATION and rhythm go hand in hand once she's picked up the beat of a catchy tune.

engrossed in a variety of play activities teaches him how to concentrate and persevere.

Play also provides an invaluable window to your child's personality. By playing with him—or watching him play with others—you will soon learn how he reacts to obstacles, failures, and victories. You'll see his quirky sense of humour emerge and his social skills begin to develop over time. His manner of playing can reveal his emotions, aptitudes, and preferred learning styles—whether

play contributes to your child's emotional, physical, and intellectual development. Through play, a toddler learns so many vital skills—how to communicate, count, and solve problems. He hones his gross motor skills by tossing balls or climbing up a slide and polishes his fine motor skills by painting with brushes or drawing with crayons. His imagination soars as he pretends to converse on a toy telephone or dons a succession of silly hats in front of a mirror. His language skills improve as he listens to stories and strives to communicate his needs and preferences. Early play encounters with his peers, siblings, parents, and other adults teach him how to get along with others and to respect rules and boundaries. Becoming

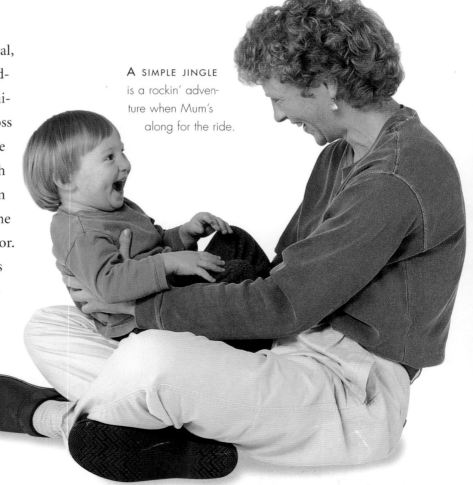

A SIMPLE JINGLE is a rockin' adventure when Mum's along for the ride.

he's responding well to verbal instructions or visual images, for example, or if he retains information best after hands-on experiences.

Play also affords a wonderful opportunity for bonding with your toddler. When she is in a quiet mood, cuddling and looking at picture books or building an elaborate block tower creates a feeling of peaceful togetherness. When she's feeling a bit rowdier, a game of hide-and-seek or a beanbag toss imparts the notion that parents can be fun as well as sources of care and compassion. When you help her acquire new skills and praise her efforts, you convincingly demonstrate how you are always there to lend support and spur her progress—and countless studies demonstrate that children learn

A FEW RUBBER BALLS can teach a toddler worlds about distance, size, and shape.

best in a loving, supportive environment. In so many ways, being your child's enthusiastic play partner creates a special closeness that will resonate throughout both of your lives.

ROLLING TO THE MUSIC lets toddlers (and mums) exercise their rambunctious sides.

DIFFERENT WAYS TO PLAY

This book is designed to help you make the most of the wonderful toddler years by providing a wealth of simple and diverse activities to enjoy with your child. You'll find rousing fingerplays to sing along to, art projects, bath-time activities, games with blankets and boxes and blocks, as well as many other imaginative suggestions. There are ways to introduce children to the joys of music, to encourage muscular coordination and strength, and to build budding vocabularies. The wide variety of activities touches upon every important component of a child's physical, mental, social, and emotional skills, and each has been carefully designed and selected for developmental appropriateness. Some are classics, some are Gymboree's own innovations, but all are designed to foster the type of loving, nurturing interaction that helps a toddler learn and forms a lasting bond between parent and child.

Although playing and learning are inextricably linked, the point of these activities is not to run your toddler through a rigid battery of exercises. Instead, *Toddler Play*'s emphasis is on having fun first and foremost through activities that also happen to spur age-appropriate development in your child. These activities help build a solid foundation for all future learning. In other words, they help your toddler learn *how* to learn.

READY, SET, PLAY!

Far from being rigid, the instructions in this book are intended as guidelines for loosely structured play, open to modification as you respond to your own child's particular interests and inclinations. Get things going, then step back and allow your toddler the freedom to explore

and experiment as he wishes. This is key to encouraging him to work things out on his own, learn to problem-solve, think creatively, and achieve self-esteem and a sense of autonomy.

Setting up a well-designed, safe play environment also contributes to his growing sense of independence and provides stimulation: deck the walls in his room with shatterproof mirrors and colourful

BRING ON THE NONSENSE—no song is too silly as far as your giggly wiggle-worm is concerned.

17

•INTRODUCTION•

This book's activities are grouped chronologically in six-month age bands that match key stages in a child's development. The age bands are general guidelines only, as there is a wide range of developmental differences among children.

12 MONTHS AND UP

Whether they're crawling, cruising, or walking, one-year-olds enjoy a newfound mobility that accompanies their enormous curiosity about the world. Their fine motor skills have developed to the point where they can assuredly pick up small objects and stack a few blocks. They love listening to their parents' voices, such as when reading a story or singing a song. They understand many words and respond to some simple commands; most also begin saying a few words of their own.

18 MONTHS AND UP

Children this age are determined to explore, handle, taste, and shake, rattle, and roll everything in sight. Their increasingly sophisticated gross motor skills allow them to walk, run, and climb, and their fine motor skills permit them to eat with a spoon and throw a ball. They enjoy games that engage their tactile senses and can express an appreciation of music by swaying. Their vocabulary averages more than a dozen words, and they can usually form simple two- and three-word phrases.

24 MONTHS AND UP

Children's strength, flexibility, and balance are stronger and surer now: they can unscrew the lid of a jar and perform other tasks that showcase their developing fine motor abilities. Their enthusiasm for music continues, and they are beginning to use their imaginations. Most enjoy the company of peers, although rather than engaging in joint activities, they tend to play independently side by side. Two-year-olds might have more than two hundred words in their vocabulary and they begin to speak in simple sentences.

30 MONTHS AND UP

Older toddlers delight in activities that refine and stretch their physical abilities, such as running, jumping, tricycle riding, and playing a simple game of catch. They continue to hone their fine motor skills, such as holding a crayon or paintbrush. Their attention spans increase, and they often show a passion for classifying activities and sorting games. Their fluency with language grows dramatically, and they catch on to the notion of abstractions, making for a rich repertoire of fantasy play.

18

posters, and transform the ceiling into a starry sky or an undersea fantasy with glow-in-the-dark stickers. Arrange low bookcases or tables with a rotating assortment of toddler-friendly toys, books, and art supplies, providing bins for easy sorting and storage. Place a hamper within your child's reach, as well as a rack for hanging up clothes. Most important, don't think you need to stock up on a lot of expensive and elaborate playthings; classics such as puzzles, bubbles, puppets, blocks, tops, and balls remain versatile and engaging toddler toys.

As you become familiar with *Toddler Play,* feel free to return again and again to your child's favourite activities. Children benefit greatly from repetition. It allows them to test and refine what they have learned and it gives them a sense of accomplishment (for more on repetition, see page 52). And don't fret if your child doesn't seem to conform to the age bands listed—if your one-year-old, for instance, is having trouble handling the beach ball in Pass the Ball or, conversely, if your two-year-old quickly memorizes every song and fingerplay in the book. Keep in mind that each child develops at her

own pace and in her own style (for more information on developmental differences, see page 34). The age bands are simply broad guidelines, and there are plenty of activities in this book to suit every child's unique needs and preferences.

So go ahead, put on your play clothes, warm up those vocal cords, and prepare to enter and enhance your toddler's world by trying the activities suggested in the following pages. They'll help you provide a richer, more stimulating environment for your child—and a treasury of happy memories for you, your child's first playmate.

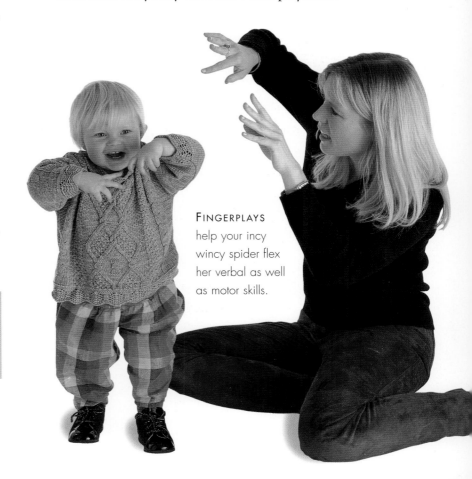

FINGERPLAYS help your incy wincy spider flex her verbal as well as motor skills.

PLEASE NOTE To avoid showing a preference for either gender, use of the male and female pronouns is varied throughout this book and generally corresponds to the sex of the child shown in any accompanying photograph.

PLAY ACTIVITIES

THE FOLLOWING PAGES contain more than one hundred activities, all designed to please and challenge toddlers and make the most of their favourite time of day: the time you spend playing together. You'll find suggestions for every type of meaningful play, from funny fingerplays and nature walks to art sessions and building projects, so you can choose the activities that best suit your child's mood and interests. All these loosely structured, open-ended games can be enjoyed with a minimum amount of equipment and a maximum amount of imagination. So flip through these pages, see what new adventure you and your toddler are ready for, and let the fun begin!

A GUIDE TO ACTIVITIES

HOW TO USE THIS BOOK

IF YOU'RE LIKE most parents of toddlers, you're probably long on love but short on time. Consequently, *Toddler Play* offers a number of quick-reference features so busy parents can learn about playtime activities at a glance. The features in this book are designed to ensure that each activity is easy to find, simple to understand, and quick to implement—allowing you to spend less time reading directions and more time having fun with your child.

Parental Tips *offer insight into your child's development and valuable advice on being your child's first teacher and playmate.*

Colour photographs *of toddlers—often paired with one of their parents—demonstrate each activity in the book.*

Lyrics appear *on a yellow background with each song, chant, and rhyme and frequently include hand and body motions.*

22

For ease of reference, *every game is categorized by type—from art projects to ball games to water play—so you can quickly find an activity that matches your child's specific interests.*

Each activity *includes concise, easy-to-follow instructions as well as information on how to vary activities and, where appropriate, how to adapt them to appeal to your child as he grows.*

Age labels *show the recommended optimum starting age for each activity. This book is divided into four age ranges (for more details on the developmental stages associated with each age, see page 18). The labels provide a broad guide to help you find an appropriate activity for your child; most activities can be adapted successfully for any toddler between one and three years of age.*

Skill Spotlights *explain the developmental focus of each game and contain quick-reference checklists of the activity's primary benefits.*

Making Your Own *provides suggestions on how to fashion makeshift toys and props from inexpensive, everyday materials.*

Cross-references *point to related activities that your child might also enjoy because of similarity in topic or spirit.*

Research Reports *highlight recent scientific findings that reveal how young children develop and learn over the years.*

PASS THE BALL

BALL PLAY·FOR BEGINNERS

SKILLSPOTLIGHT

Learning to roll *or even stop a ball helps toddlers refine their gross motor skills and develop eye-hand (or eye-foot, as the case may be) coordination. It also helps them develop a sense of timing as they attempt to figure out how long it will take before the ball reaches them.*

Body Awareness	✔
Coordination	✔
Gross Motor Skills	✔

IF YOUR CHILD ENJOYS THIS ACTIVITY, also try Tube Tricks, page 96. ▶

F EW TODDLERS can actually catch a ball—that takes a good bit of coordination—but most love to push, kick, and grab this engaging toy. To start your toddler out on ball play, choose a flat, grassy spot outside or a cleared space inside, and sit just a couple of feet away from her. Gently roll the ball to your child and encourage her to roll it back in your direction. As she gets better at it, sit farther and farther away. Try softly bouncing the ball between the two of you, as well.

A BALL THAT'S ABOUT THE SIZE of your child's head is just right; it's not so big that it will overwhelm her and not so small that she'll have trouble handling it.

12 MONTHS
1
AND UP

THE FINGER BAND

A SONG WITH IMAGINARY INSTRUMENTS

IT'S NEVER TOO EARLY to give your toddler music lessons, especially when the instruments are make-believe. Don't worry if your child has never heard a clarinet, much less seen a trombone—she will enjoy watching and imitating your hand movements, whatever they are. Make your gestures distinct and energetic. If at first she can't copy you, move her hands and fingers for her. As she gets more coordinated and is able to imitate you, march your legs up and down as you sing and play. Try alternating between singing softly and loudly, explaining the difference as you do so.

PROP YOUR LITTLE MAJORETTE on your lap and introduce her to your finger band before launching into this musical parade.

 to the *tune* of **"The Mulberry Bush"**

Hold your fingers up and wiggle them for the first verse, then pantomime playing the instruments for the following verses.

The finger band has come to town, come to town, come to town, the finger band has come to town, so early in the morning.

The finger band can play the drums, play the drums, play the drums, the finger band can play the drums, so early in the morning.

The finger band can play the flute, play the flute, play the flute, the finger band can play the flute, so early in the morning.

Continue the song with additional instruments: cymbals, clarinet, piano, trombone, guitar, violin, and so on.

✓ **Eye-Hand Coordination**

✓ **Language Development**

✓ **Listening Skills**

25

PARACHUTE PLAY

FUN WAYS TO BUILD BALANCING SKILLS

SKILLSPOTLIGHT

Parachute play *enhances your toddler's ability to balance—a skill that translates to freedom and independence, because it's a precursor to walking, running, and more complex physical actions such as skipping or even doing a somersault. Parachutes are also intrinsically interesting items to use because of their slick feel and bold colours; reinforce your child's colour-recognition skills by naming the colours as you play.*

Balance	✔
Tactile Stimulation	✔
Visual Discrimination	✔

YOUR TODDLER will no doubt cheer as you treat him to a slip-and-slide parachute ride, and in the process you'll safely challenge his ability to balance while in motion. On a carpeted floor, seat or lay him on a colourful mini-parachute, blanket, or sheet, then gently—and gradually—pull him around, taking care to avoid any furniture and sharp corners as you explore the great indoors.

• Recruit another adult to help you hold the blanket or parachute over your child's head. If your child can stand with ease, test his balance by slowly raising and lowering the parachute while he stands underneath it and admires the colours or pattern. Do this carefully; even a lightweight parachute can topple an unsteady toddler.

WHO NEEDS A MAGIC CARPET? Being transported by Daddy on a colourful parachute, sheet, or blanket is a toddler's dream come true.

26

12 MONTHS
1
AND UP

"Here we go!"

● Walking in a circle, hold the blanket or parachute over your toddler's head singing "Ring-a-Ring of Roses" (see Circle Songs, page 114, for the lyrics) or another appropriate song that your child likes. At the end of the song, let the parachute float down to the floor over your toddler. This is a particularly fun activity when a group of kids joins in the merriment.

IF YOUR CHILD ENJOYS THIS ACTIVITY, also try Freeze Dance, page 39. ▶

RHYME TIME

NURSERY RHYMES have been engaging young children for centuries. Even when they don't make sense, there's something infectious and wonderful about the rhyming words. Rhymes also make language more interesting and memorable, and they help you talk to your toddler on a level you can both enjoy. Don't hesitate to create your own hand movements or gestures to complement some of the following favourite nursery rhymes.

LITTLE BO-PEEP

Little Bo-Peep has lost her sheep and
doesn't know where to find them.
Leave them alone
and they'll come home,
bringing their tails behind them.

HUMPTY DUMPTY

Humpty Dumpty sat on a wall,
Humpty Dumpty had a great fall.
All the king's horses
and all the king's men
couldn't put Humpty together again.

JACK BE NIMBLE

Jack be nimble,
Jack be quick.
Jack jump over
the candlestick!

JACK AND JILL

Jack and Jill went up a hill
to fetch a pail of water.
Jack fell down and broke his crown,
and Jill came tumbling after.

ROUND AND ROUND

**Round and round the garden
goes the little bear.**
*set your toddler in front of you and run
your finger in a circle around his tummy*
One, two, three, four,
*gently squeeze each hand and foot,
one on each count*
tickle under there!
tickle your toddler under the chin

LITTLE MISS MUFFET

Little Miss Muffet sat on a tuffet
set your child on your lap
eating her curds and whey.
pretend to feed him from a bowl
Along came a spider
crawl your hand toward him like a spider
and sat down beside her
set your "spider" hand on his lap
and frightened Miss Muffet away!
holding your child, jump off your seat

HICKORY DICKORY DOCK

Hickory dickory dock,
*move your index fingers from side
to side, mimicking a ticking clock*
the mouse ran up the clock.
run two fingers up your child's arm
The clock struck one,
hold up one finger
the mouse ran down.
run fingers down your child's arm
Hickory dickory dock!
mimic the ticking clock

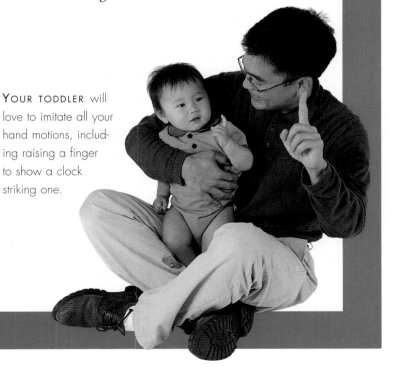

YOUR TODDLER will
love to imitate all your
hand motions, includ-
ing raising a finger
to show a clock
striking one.

29

BUBBLE BURSTERS

A POP-THE-BUBBLE GAME OF CHASE

SKILLSPOTLIGHT

Chasing, catching, *and popping bubbles contribute to eye-hand coordination, sensory stimulation, body awareness, and gross motor skills. And if your toddler tries to blow bubbles herself, she'll learn about cause and effect. Your bubble burster is also discovering that when she touches an apparently solid object, it sometimes pops—her first lesson in physics!*

Eye-Hand Coordination	✔
Gross Motor Skills	✔
Language Development	✔
Tactile Stimulation	✔

MAKING YOUR OWN

For the soap solution, mix 1 cup of water, 1 tablespoon of glycerin (available in most chemists), and 2 tablespoons of washing-up liquid. Fashion bubble wands from pipe cleaners, plastic bag ties, even plastic cups with the bottom cut out.

IF THERE IS A MAGIC EQUATION for entrancing a toddler, it must be the combination of a simple soap solution and a bubble wand. Blowing, chasing, and popping bubbles is an excellent opportunity to encourage movement, stimulate eye-hand coordination, and introduce the concepts of big and small, high and low. Experiment with an assortment of bubble wands in varying sizes. Don't be surprised if your toddler enjoys this activity so much that "bubble" becomes one of her favourite words!

• Use a large wand to make big bubbles and cheer her as she chases and pops them, then repeat the activity with a smaller wand. Blow forcefully when you're creating a shower of tiny bubbles and softly when you're making a huge bubble. Blow the bubbles up high and down low, saying "high" or "low" as they float away.

• Take your child outdoors and blow bubbles. Explain that the wind that rustles the leaves and blows her hair also carries the bubbles away. Urge your toddler to pop the bubbles with her fingers or stomp on them with her feet. Walk backwards as you blow on the bubble wand so she'll chase you to catch the bubbles.

A BIG SHOWER OF BUBBLES will fascinate your little one. And when she chases and pops them, she'll be exercising her coordination and gross motor skills.

CLAP, CLAP, CLAP

A MOVE-YOUR-BODY SONG

SKILL SPOTLIGHT

Learning the words *for body parts, and learning to control those hands, arms, and feet, is serious business for kids this age. While your toddler may already be pointing to her body parts when you name them, this song gives her a chance to practise isolating and moving her hands, feet, arms, and lips.*

Body Awareness	✔
Gross Motor Skills	✔
Listening Skills	✔
Social Skills	✔

IF YOUR CHILD ENJOYS THIS ACTIVITY, also try Just Like Me, page 57. ▶

IF YOU'RE FAMILIAR with the ever-popular song "The Wheels on the Bus," you can add a new twist to the tune with these lyrics. "Clap, Clap, Clap" coaxes your little one to coordinate body movements with words. And associating words and actions with a melody and a beat will enhance her understanding of rhythm, because she'll be able to feel it and mimic it with her body.

• Young toddlers are eager to learn the words for body parts, so be sure to emphasize those words in the song—"hands," "arms," "mouth"—by enunciating them or singing them more loudly. Make big motions at first to underscore the meaning of the words.

• There's plenty of room for variation: ask her to tap her knees, shake her hips, or nod her head.

• After she's learned the song, make a few innocent "mistakes"—clap your hands when you're supposed to be tapping your foot, for instance—and watch her squeal with laughter. Your child already has a sense of humour.

YOUR TODDLER WILL ENJOY imitating you as you clap your hands and tap your foot in this simple music game.

12 MONTHS
1
AND UP

 to the *tune* of **"The Wheels on the Bus"**

You take your little hands
and go clap, clap, clap,
clap your hands
clap, clap, clap,
clap, clap, clap.
You take your little hands
and go clap, clap, clap,
clap your little hands.

You take your little foot
and go tap, tap, tap,
tap your child's foot for her
tap, tap, tap,
tap, tap, tap.
You take your little foot
and go tap, tap, tap,
tap your little foot.

You take your little arms
and go hug, hug, hug,
hug each other
hug, hug, hug,
hug, hug, hug.

You take your little arms
and go hug, hug, hug,
hug your mum and dad.

You take your little mouth
and go kiss, kiss, kiss,
pucker your lips
kiss, kiss, kiss,
kiss, kiss, kiss.
You take your little mouth
and go kiss, kiss, kiss,
kiss your mum and dad.

You take your little hand
and wave bye, bye, bye,
wave good-bye
bye, bye, bye,
bye, bye, bye.
You take your little hand
and wave bye, bye, bye,
wave your little hand.

AT THEIR OWN PACE

BABIES SIT UP at six months. They utter their first "dada" at nine. They crawl at seven months and walk at age one. When parents are confronted by the firm developmental timetables sometimes espoused in popular child-care books, they often are pleased if their children achieve a milestone a few weeks or months ahead of schedule—and panicked if their offspring are late. But while pediatricians used to treat these timetables as if they were carved in granite, most practitioners today agree that there is a much wider developmental range in perfectly healthy children.

A child may first roll over, for example, at any time from two to six months of age. Children can vary the age at which they start talking by a year or more, and future soccer stars may take their first steps as early as eight months and as late as eighteen. Although children generally follow the prescribed developmental sequence, some will skip a milestone completely—they might never learn to crawl, for example. Instead, when their muscle tone and coordination skills are ready, they just get up and start walking.

All of these developmental milestones are a matter of complex neural and muscular maturation, which is affected by both inherited and environmental factors—a child may walk late in life, for example, if the family has a history of late walkers. Often a child lags in one area while accelerating in another. In rare instances, a delayed milestone can signal significant problems, but in the vast majority of cases, it's just a matter of a child developing at her own rate. As educational psychologist Jane Healy observes in her book *Your Child's Growing Mind:* "A child who is lagging slightly in development is on the same track as the others. His train simply goes at a slower pace, although it stands every chance of reaching the same destination." ■

INCY WINCY SPIDER

A FAVOURITE FIRST FINGERPLAY

IN THIS POPULAR SONG, you can portray the trials of the hapless incy wincy spider with fun-to-mimic hand motions. By repeating the song and the gestures you are not only entertaining your toddler, you're also stimulating her listening and language skills. You can bolster the activity by crawling the spider up your child's tummy, "pouring" the rain down over her shoulders, and crossing her arms above her head to make the sun. When she seems proficient, try singing the song and cuing her to perform the finger movements—eventually she may surprise you with a solo rendition.

The incy wincy spider went up the water spout,
walk your fingers up in the air

down came the rain and washed the spider out.
wiggle your fingers downward to make rain

Out came the sun and dried up all the rain,
form a circle with your fingers above your head

and the incy wincy spider went up the spout again.
walk your fingers up again

✔ **Fine Motor Skills**

✔ **Listening Skills**

✔ **Tactile Stimulation**

MIMING THE TRAVAILS of the incy wincy spider with you not only promotes your toddler's listening and language abilities, it helps her develop her fine motor skills.

35

THE PILLOW COURSE

FIRST STEPS ON A PATH OF PILLOWS

SKILLSPOTLIGHT

Movement and exploration *are near and dear to a toddler's heart, so an opportunity to move around in an interesting environment is bound to be met with joy. This activity is also an excellent way for your toddler to build his motor skills by challenging large muscle groups and to increase both his balance and coordination as he faces and overcomes unexpected physical obstacles.*

Balance	✔
Body Awareness	✔
Eye-Foot Coordination	✔
Gross Motor Skills	✔

CREATE A SIMPLE, safe obstacle course in your living room or family room by laying out a path of pillows and cushions. Allow the course to zigzag around the room.

• Encourage your child to complete the course by crawling or walking along the path. It will be a bumpy, lumpy route, so even if he's already walking be sure to hold on to his hand as he begins the journey. Once he becomes more surefooted, let him take some steps on the pillows by himself, but stay nearby just in case he starts to topple. Remove your toddler's shoes and socks to help him keep his balance.

• Vary the height of the path by stacking a couple of pillows. You can make the course more challenging by running it under a table so he has to crawl underneath, or by positioning the pillows around the room (avoid furniture with sharp edges) so he must manoeuvre around footstools and upholstered chairs or sofas.

• Use cushions and pillows of varying sizes, colours, and textures to keep the course interesting. Don't be surprised if your young athlete stops occasionally to feel the obstacles with his hands or feet. Allow him to explore, then gently encourage him to keep going.

....
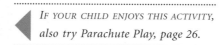
IF YOUR CHILD ENJOYS THIS ACTIVITY,
also try Parachute Play, page 26.
....

36

HE'S ON THE WAY
to walking when he follows
a trail of cushions around
the house—with Daddy's
help, of course.

RESEARCH REPORT

The wide range *in age at which
children begin walking—any time
from seven to eighteen months—
reflects the complexity of this deceptively simple act. The mind as
well as the body is involved in ven-
turing those first steps, and it takes
time for nerve cells to operate
smoothly, allowing deliberate and
controlled movement. A child also
must build up sufficient muscle
tone in his legs and hone his sense
of balance and coordination, skills
toddlers acquire at different rates.*

HATS ON!

EXPERIMENTING WITH DIFFERENT HEADGEAR

SKILLSPOTLIGHT

Talking to your toddler *about the hats the two of you are wearing helps expose him to new words that will someday become a part of his vocabulary. And seeing you in different hats teaches him that you're still Mummy even if you look a little different. When your child is a bit older, he'll start to role-play with the hats, a game that will stretch his capacity for imaginative play.*

Concept Development	✔
Language Development	✔
Social Skills	✔

YOUR TODDLER WILL MARVEL at your elaborate headdress and smile when you make him a fireman—especially if you mimic special sound effects, such as an engine siren, to go with each hat.

YOUR YOUNG ONE GRINS when you put your baseball cap on backward. Now watch his face light up as you put a parade of special hats on his head, too. Pick up fun gear at charity shops and perhaps in Grandma's attic. Then try it on and giggle together in front of a mirror. This is a good opportunity to help expand your child's vocabulary by using adjectives to describe the hats ("This big hat is red." or "The feathers are so soft.").

• As your toddler gets closer to age two, he'll be able to revel in role-playing as he tries on different hats.

FREEZE DANCE

STOP-AND-GO MUSICAL FUN

PLAY AN AUDIOTAPE OR CD and put a friend in charge of the volume control while you take your young dancer for a twirl—or record your own tape with sudden silences. Hold your toddler in your arms; when the music starts, exaggerate your dance moves by swaying from side to side and "dipping" her on occasion. When the music stops, hold your stance; begin dancing when the music starts again, then "freeze" each time it halts. Older toddlers may be able to dance—and stop—on their own, but most are just as happy to "freeze" in your embrace.

SKILLSPOTLIGHT

By taking a ride *in your arms as you dance the night away, your toddler experiences the rhythm of music, a crucial first step in developing both language and music skills. And when you freeze in mid-action, she learns to balance herself in your arms. Suddenly turning the music on and off gives your toddler something she dearly loves—a surprise—and cultivates listening skills as well.*

✔ **Balance**

✔ **Listening Skills**

✔ **Social Skills**

CHA-CHA-CHA . . . Swinging to the beat of the music is a surefire way to thrill your toddler—especially when you surprise her with sudden pauses in your boogie.

39

TWINKLE, TWINKLE

SOME SONGS ENDURE generation after generation, giving parents and grandparents a chance to share their old favourites with young children. But old favourites can be changed in new and surprising ways, so as you sing these suggested variations of "Twinkle, Twinkle Little Star," try to come up with some simple—or silly—improvisations of your own.

SHE'LL BE ENCHANTED when you sing and mime the old standby "Twinkle, Twinkle Little Star"—but there are countless variations if you want to try new lyrics.

TWINKLE, TWINKLE LITTLE STAR

Twinkle, twinkle little star,
hold hands up, opening and closing fists
how I wonder what you are!

Up above the world so high,
point upward
like a diamond in the sky.
create a diamond with thumbs and forefingers

Twinkle, twinkle little star,
open and close fists
how I wonder what you are!

40

THE APPLE TREE

 to the ***tune*** *of* **"Twinkle, Twinkle Little Star"**

Way up high in the apple tree
stretch arms up high
two little apples
looking down at me.
make circles around eyes with thumbs
and forefingers

I shook that tree
just as hard as I could,
shake an imaginary tree with
both hands
down came the apples
float fingers down
and "mmm" they were good!
rub tummy and smile

I shook that tree
just as hard as I could,
shake an imaginary tree with
both hands
down came the apples
float fingers down
and "mmm" they were good!
rub tummy and smile

THE SKY SO BLUE

 to the ***tune*** *of* **"Twinkle, Twinkle Little Star"**

Way up in the sky so blue
reach up to the sky with both hands
two little clouds said "peekaboo."
play peekaboo with hands

The wind blew the clouds
just as hard as it could,
rub hands together and shiver
down came the raindrops
flutter fingers down
and "oooh". . . they felt good!

The wind blew the clouds
just as hard as it could,
rub hands together
and shiver
down came the raindrops
flutter fingers down
and "oooh". . . they felt good!

41

THE WHEELS ON THE BUS

A MUSICAL TRANSPORTATION TOUR

SKILL SPOTLIGHT

The catchy tune *and easy-to-follow gestures make this sing-along a skill-building activity for all toddlers. Repeating the song stimulates your toddler's auditory development, while the hand movements help him conceptualize what the words mean. As his motor skills and memory improve, he will readily imitate most of the hand gestures and even begin to anticipate them.*

Body Awareness	✔
Concept Development	✔
Coordination	✔
Language Development	✔
Listening Skills	✔

THIS SONG is an all-time toddler classic. You can perform it in many ways, but it's easiest with your child seated facing you or on your lap facing away from you. If he's propped up on your lap, gently guide his hands through the movements.

• Begin by showing him the different motions as you sing, then encourage him to join in.

• Don't be afraid to improvise with new verses and corresponding hand movements if the spirit moves you—your toddler will love it!

TAKE A FAVOURITE PASSENGER for a ride on the bus, showing him how the wheels go round and round and the wipers go swish, swish, swish.

The wheels on the bus go round and round,
roll forearms forward in a circular motion

round and round,
continue to roll arms

round and round.
roll arms

The wheels on the bus go round and round,
roll arms

all through the town.
draw a circle in the air

The horn on the bus goes beep, beep, beep,
press imaginary horn with hand

beep, beep, beep,
press horn with hand

beep, beep, beep.
press horn with hand

The horn on the bus goes beep, beep, beep,
press horn with hand

all through the town.
draw a circle in the air

Continue with:
The wipers on the bus go swish, swish, swish . . .
sway forearms back and forth

The driver on the bus says "Move on back" . . .
point over your shoulder with your thumb

The lights on the bus go blink, blink, blink . . .
open and close fists

The baby on the bus goes waah, waah, waah . . .
make cradling motion with your arms

The parents on the bus say I love you . . .
hug your child

IF YOUR CHILD ENJOYS THIS ACTIVITY, also try Incy Wincy Spider, page 35.

12 MONTHS AND UP

BAND ON THE RUN

MUSIC FROM THE KITCHEN CABINET

SKILLSPOTLIGHT

One way toddlers learn *cause and effect is by making sounds with a variety of objects. As a child bangs on a bowl, he learns that he is capable of creating sounds by himself. As he practises, he improves his coordination and his understanding of rhythm, and as he experiments with the various "instruments" in his cabinet, he learns that he can create a myriad of interesting sounds.*

Cause & Effect	✔
Coordination	✔
Listening Skills	✔
Rhythm Exploration	✔

CLEAR OUT A KITCHEN CUPBOARD (near the floor) for your child and fill it with sturdy wooden spoons, metal bowls of different sizes, lightweight pans (cake pans and small frying pans work well), wooden salad bowls, metal lids of various sizes, and plastic measuring cups. The greater the variety of "instruments," the greater the variety of sounds you and your toddler will be able to make, so be creative as you stock the cupboard. If you have toy instruments on hand, add them to the mix.

• With older toddlers, create a stop-and-go band. Have your child bang on the "instruments" while listening to you—the bandleader—give directions to stop the music and start it again.

• As your young musician plays, encourage him to experiment with sound by banging in different ways: with enthusiasm, gently, slowly, fast. Be sure to demonstrate to show him the difference.

• Play one of his favourite music tapes or CDs (tunes with a strong beat are best) and encourage him to add his own percussion sounds.

EVERYTHING BUT THE KITCHEN SINK—and that would probably work as well—is a potential instrument for a budding musician.

The raucous noise *that results from your toddler's kitchen concert is actually good "brain food," says educational psychologist Jane Healy. "Toys with sound or visual input improve cognitive skills, but it is important that [your child] be able to interact with them. Banging two pans together is far better . . . than pushing buttons to create noises produced by hidden electronic parts. The child should be able to link cause and effect— and see the parts of the toy at work."*

45

PEEKABOO BOXES

PUTTING NAMES TO FAMILIAR FACES

This activity refines *your child's visual memory and fine motor skills. Most significantly, matching a word with its visual representation helps build the language skills he'll need later, when he begins reading and writing. As your child's vocabulary expands, surprise him now and then by pasting new pictures inside the boxes.*

Fine Motor Skills	✔
Language Development	✔
Social Skills	✔
Visual Memory	✔

COLLECT AN ASSORTMENT of cigar boxes, shoe boxes, or boxes from gift stores. Cut out pictures of family members or easily recognizable objects (household items, animals, toys) and paste one inside the lid of each box. Open the boxes and discuss the images inside. As your child's confidence grows, ask him to open the boxes and name the pictures. Once he masters this (around two years of age), test his memory: ask him which box contains the picture of Daddy, a horse, or a ball.

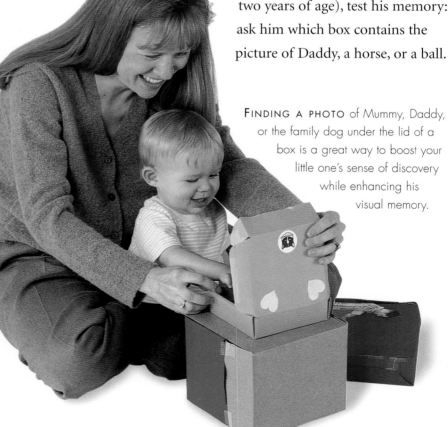

FINDING A PHOTO of Mummy, Daddy, or the family dog under the lid of a box is a great way to boost your little one's sense of discovery while enhancing his visual memory.

46

12 MONTHS
1
AND UP

FUNNY FEET

EXPLORING TEXTURE WITH YOUR TOES

EVEN A CHILD who has been toddling for several months is still getting used to the sensations involved in walking. Take advantage of her curiosity by removing her shoes and leading her outside across a variety of textures, such as warm sand, smooth pebbles, cool concrete, wet grass, and gooey mud. As she gets older, ask her what she feels as she's walking. If she doesn't know the words yet, suggest some: "warm," "prickly," "soft." If you're worried about dirty feet, stomping in a basin of warm, soapy water will continue the game.

YOUR TODDLER WILL DELIGHT in the feel of different textures, such as soft grass, on her sensitive soles. Take off your shoes and join in the fun!

SKILL SPOTLIGHT

Walking barefoot *is easier for your young toddler than walking with shoes because she can use her tiny toes to help with balance. And while the sensations of walking on unusual surfaces may make her giggle, she'll start to grasp the properties associated with different materials, as well as a few words to describe them.*

✔	**Body Awareness**
✔	**Language Development**
✔	**Sensory Exploration**
✔	**Tactile Discrimination**

CARDBOARD COTTAGES

CREATING A PINT-SIZE PLAY WORLD

SKILLSPOTLIGHT

Creeping through tunnels
fosters motor coordination and spatial awareness, while playing house and peekaboo with Mummy or Daddy encourages social skills. Choosing decorations helps older toddlers learn to discuss likes and dislikes and to express their artistic talents.

Gross Motor Skills	✔
Sensory Exploration	✔
Social Skills	✔
Tactile Stimulation	✔

MAKING YOUR OWN

Rectangular boxes make good tunnels; square boxes make nice cottages. Decorate the cottages with coloured paper and pens to make them more inviting. Just be sure to keep the "floor" of the box on the bottom so it won't collapse.

YOUR TODDLER'S GREATEST joy is trying to be independent; her greatest frustration is not being big enough, strong enough, or "allowed enough" to be all she would like to be. A town made of cardboard boxes makes a toddler the master of her own universe, and it's easy enough for you to build. Place boxes end to end to create tunnels for crawling and hiding, and use appliance or large packing boxes to make perfect playhouses.

• Cut door and window flaps in the sides of boxes so your toddler can open and shut them. Play "bye-bye" and peekaboo games as she looks out so she can practise being independent while you're still close by.

• Turn boxes into sensory centres by laying differently textured carpet scraps inside, leaving musical toys in corners, and providing baskets of colourful objects to empty and refill.

IF YOUR CHILD ENJOYS THIS ACTIVITY, also try Hide-and-Seek, page 78.

12 MONTHS
1
AND UP

"Hello! Is anybody home?"

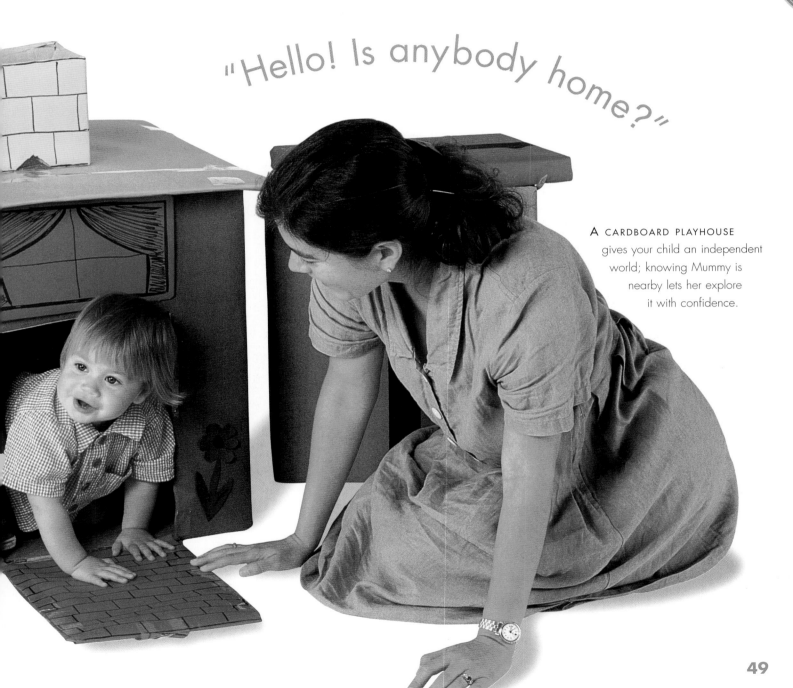

A CARDBOARD PLAYHOUSE gives your child an independent world; knowing Mummy is nearby lets her explore it with confidence.

49

PICTURE THIS

GROWING A BOOKWORM

SKILLSPOTLIGHT

Reading is an important tool *for learning language. Toddlers learn most of the rules of grammar simply by hearing you and others speak. And recent studies show that the size of a toddler's vocabulary depends on how much speech she hears in a meaningful context. So the more you read to your child, the easier it will be for her to develop strong language skills.*

Language Development	✔
Listening Skills	✔
Visual Discrimination	✔
Visual Memory	✔

SHE MAY NOT BE ABLE to talk and she may not understand all your words, but even a young toddler loves to "read books" with a parent or grandparent. The rhythm of the words engages her; the pictures teach her about her world.

• Choose books with clear pictures of familiar objects and point them out to your child as you read. It will help her learn the words for everyday things, such as "chair," "house," and "car."

• Select books made of cloth, plastic, or heavy cardboard. They can withstand toddlers' eager hands and mouths more readily than paper. And small books with padded covers are easier for little hands to handle.

• Edit out long narratives and hard words. Instead, abridge the plot and spend time talking about the illustrations or photographs. That will keep her interested and help her develop observational skills.

• Emphasize the rhymes and funny words that will engage her.

• Remember, toddlers can't sit still for long periods of time, so tailor your reading session to her attention span. Let her wander off to play with her toys or be with her own thoughts when she wants to. Ending the session while it's still fun will ensure that you're building a positive association with reading that will last a lifetime.

EVEN A CHILD who is too young to understand the plot will delight in the colourful pictures, the simple rhymes, and the cadence of Gran's voice.

Although teachers *often exhort parents to read to their school-age children, a 1994 report by the Carnegie Corporation found that only half of all American babies and toddlers receive this attention. Yet early exposure to these important tools of learning and pleasure, as Penelope Leach writes in* Your Baby and Child, *helps children "to make friends with [books] and learn to value them." She recommends that parents introduce their toddler to a variety of both picture and story books, and suggests they spend a lot of time talking about the illustrations. "'Reading' pictures," Leach explains, "is a necessary start toward reading text."*

REPETITION IN PLAY

THINK YOU'LL GO nuts if you have to spend another minute rolling a ball back and forth with your toddler? Bored with reading his favourite book over and over again? Or maybe you're just worried that your child needs more variety in his play and you feel you should try to keep him from returning again and again to a few preferred activities.

Although it may try your patience, never underestimate the value of repetition when it comes to a child's development. As educational psychologist Jane Healy says in her book *Your Child's Growing Mind,* "An activity must be repeated many times to firm up neural networks for proficiency." In other words, by repeating the same story to your child every evening you are helping to stimulate the brain cells that allow your child to make the association between words and the objects they represent. And when it comes to rolling that ball, you'll soon see how his eye-hand coordination improves. A simple activity such as this helps prime him for more complex tasks in coming years, whether it's understanding the nuances in James Joyce's *Ulysses* or playing professional football.

Besides, kids don't get bored as easily as adults do. As neurologist Ann Barnet notes in *The Youngest Minds,* "Nursery rhymes and simple games enthrall small children precisely because they become familiar." Mastering a new skill gives them a lot of confidence and even whets their appetites for future challenges.

This isn't to say that parents can't overdo it by spending too much time interacting on one activity with their child—even young minds and bodies can get overtaxed. So be sure to take your cues from your child: watch for signs of frustration or restlessness, but if he's enjoying an activity, let him do it . . . over and over and over again. ■

12 MONTHS
1
AND UP

FUN-FILLED JARS

FINDING OUT WHAT'S INSIDE

COLLECT A FEW large, clear plastic jars with easy-to-remove lids. Place a favourite toy or colourful scarf inside each jar and close the lid. Ask your child to take off the lid and pull out the toy or scarf. (You might need to start this activity with loose lids so her not-so-nimble fingers can remove the toys more easily.) Your toddler will be eager to remove the toys over and over again. When you're filling the jars, be sure to select toys that are more than 4.5 cm (1¾ inches) in diameter (so there won't be a choking hazard).

A TOY INSIDE a jar provides plenty of incentive to lift off the lid.

SKILLSPOTLIGHT

Learning to remove *a lid, even if it's already unscrewed, helps your toddler develop coordination and fine motor skills. And just attempting to unscrew a lid enhances these skills as well. In this activity, success is immediately rewarded, ensuring that your toddler will want to try removing the lids again and again.*

✔	**Fine Motor Skills**
✔	**Language Development**
✔	**Social Skills**

IF YOUR CHILD ENJOYS THIS ACTIVITY,
also try Cereal Challenge, page 80.

SILLY LAP SONGS

SITTING ON A PARENT'S LAP is not a passive activity for a busy toddler. Although your lap is a safe haven for your child—a place to relax and cuddle between activities—it's also associated with such pleasures as reading, rocking, bouncing . . . or singing the following songs and pretending to be an aeroplane, a pony, or even a funny frog.

THE AIRPLANE SONG

 to the *tune* of **"Row, Row, Row Your Boat"**

**Fly, fly, fly your plane,
fly your plane up high.
Merrily, merrily, merrily, merrily,
high up in the sky!**

Hold your child firmly with both hands and raise him overhead as if he were a flying aeroplane.

MAKE YOUR TODDLER feel secure as he soars like a plane by looking at him, smiling, and having as much fun as he is.

DOWN BY THE BANKS

Down by the banks of the hanky panky,
where the bullfrogs jump
from bank to banky.
They went oops, opps, belly flops.
One missed the lily pad
and went . . . kerplop!

*Bounce your child on your lap as you teach
her this chant; holding her securely, let her
"slip" partway between your legs on "kerplop."*

TROT LITTLE PONY

 "Hush Little Baby"

Trot little pony, trot to town,
trot little pony, don't slow down.
Don't spill the buttermilk,
don't spill the eggs,
trot little pony, trot to town.

*Holding your toddler securely on
your lap, bounce her up and down
as if she were riding a pony.*

WHEN WE ALL ROLL OVER

 "Have You Ever Seen a Lassie"

When we all roll over,
roll over, roll over,
when we all roll over,
how happy we'll be!

Roll this way, and that way,
and this way, and that way.
When we all roll over,
how happy we'll be!

*Bounce your toddler on your
lap as you sing, or, lying on
your back, place him facedown
on your stomach and rock him
gently from side to side.*

I HAVE A LITTLE DUCK

MAKING WAVES WITH A SONG

 to the tune of **"The Wheels on the Bus"**

**I have a little duck that says
quack, quack, quack,
quack, quack, quack,
quack, quack, quack.
I have a little duck that says
quack, quack, quack,
all day long.**
"quack" your hands to the beat

**I have a little duck that goes
splash, splash, splash,
splash, splash, splash,
splash, splash, splash.
I have a little duck that goes
splash, splash, splash,
all day long.**
splash the water to the beat

Cause & Effect	✔
Language Development	✔
Listening Skills	✔
Rhythm Exploration	✔
Sensory Exploration	✔

SHARE THIS FAMILIAR TUNE with your child as you play in the baby pool or bathtub—and use a family of rubber ducks as your colourful props. Your toddler won't need much encouragement to splash, so be sure you are both ready to get wet. In the first verse, "quack" your hands (place your palms together as if you're miming a duck bill) in the water. Little will your toddler know that in the midst of all the hilarity, you are stimulating her auditory memory and enhancing her sense of rhythm.

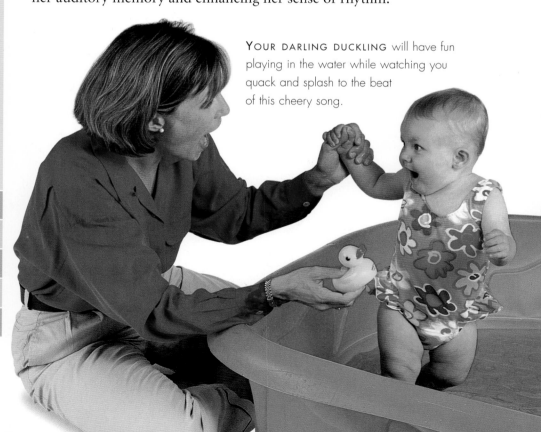

YOUR DARLING DUCKLING will have fun playing in the water while watching you quack and splash to the beat of this cheery song.

JUST LIKE ME

12 MONTHS
1
AND UP

A FOLLOW-THE-LEADER SONG

MAKE THE MOST of your toddler's natural instinct to mimic with this lively activity. Give yourself plenty of room and either sit with your child on your lap or stand facing him. Emphasize the name of each body part as you sing and point it out on your toddler's body as you make the movements. If your child is hesitant, gently help him raise and lower his arms, shoulders, and legs. Between repetitions of the song, ask him to point to his own arms or legs. Once he's following you like a pro, try adding some movements of your own invention.

SHOWING YOUR TODDLER how to make his arms go up while singing this song is a fun way to introduce him to the names of his body parts.

 to the *tune* of **"London Bridge Is Falling Down"**

Perform the actions as indicated in the lyrics.

Make your arms go up and down, up and down, up and down, make your arms go up and down, just like me.

Continue with:
**Move your hands up and down . . .
Move your shoulders up and down . . .
Flap your elbows up and down . . .
Make your legs go up and down . . .
Move your feet up and down . . .
Move your body up and down . . .**

✓ **Body Awareness**
✓ **Concept Development**
✓ **Coordination**
✓ **Creative Movement**
✓ **Listening Skills**

A STAR IS BORN

TALKING ON TAPE

SKILLSPOTLIGHT

As you may have noticed, *your toddler is quite focused on herself at this stage—and with all things belonging to her. Just as a mirror intrigues her because she can see herself, a tape recording lets her revel in the sound of her voice. This helps her develop her listening skills, which are crucial to language development.*

Language Development	✔
Listening Skills	✔
Social Skills	✔

IF YOUR CHILD ENJOYS THIS ACTIVITY, also try Mirror, Mirror, page 60. ▶

YOU'VE SEEN HOW your little one perks up at the sound of other children's voices. And you've noticed how she responds to seeing her face in the mirror. Now imagine her delight upon hearing a "reflection" of her own voice! Recording your child's voice gives her a whole new sense of herself and gives your entire family an audio "baby journal" to cherish for years to come.

• Record your toddler's sounds—laughing at Daddy's funny faces, babbling to herself as she plays, talking on her toy phone (see Ring-A-Ling, page 119), even shrieking with glee in the tub.

• Try recording a session when you read to your toddler so when she's older she can listen to your story-time voice and her own commentary.

• You can use a cassette recorder without an external microphone, but a separate, attached microphone contributes to a sharper sound. Avoid buying long tapes (those that record 120 minutes or more), since they are more likely to break and stretch over time.

• At two or three years of age, encourage your young crooner to sing several songs on tape—alone or with you if she's shy.

ONCE YOUR STARLET understands the purpose of the microphone, she'll reach for it and talk into it enthusiastically, which allows her to experience herself in a whole different way.

Recent studies show *that the size of a toddler's vocabulary depends largely on how much her caregivers talk to her. University of Chicago researcher Janellen Huttenlocher found that 20-month-olds whose mothers had the gift of the gab were shown to have about 130 more words in their vocabulary than same-age children with less talkative mums. By age two, the gap had doubled. But planting a child in front of a TV won't do: the interaction between child and speaker, and a connection to real-life events, is necessary for all of those precious words to soak in.*

12 MONTHS
1
AND UP

MIRROR, MIRROR

GETTING TO KNOW ME

SKILL SPOTLIGHT

Key to your toddler's *development is a sense of herself as a person (hence her intrigue with the notions of I and mine versus you and yours). Mirror play helps her develop this concept of self as separate from others. Toddlers are also intrigued with their bodies; labelling the parts of her body in front of the mirror helps her understand the names of those parts and encourages her to further explore her own identity.*

Body Awareness	✔
Language Development	✔
Self-Concept	✔
Social Skills	✔
Visual Discrimination	✔

YOUR CHILD has no doubt been fascinated with her own image since she was a wee baby. But mirror fun *really* begins in toddlerhood, because now she understands that the image is of herself—and understanding herself and all her body parts are her primary interests.

Sit or stand together in front of a mirror and make faces—happy, sad, and goofy. With an older toddler, encourage her to follow suit. Then point out her arms, legs, eyes, nose, and other body parts. Point out your own, as well.

Ask her who's the baby and who's the mummy—pretty soon she'll surprise you by pointing to the right image.

WATCHING HER REFLECTION in a large mirror supports your toddler's growing awareness that she is indeed a real person, with arms, eyes, and a happy face.

HEY MR. KNICKERBOCKER

12 MONTHS AND UP 1

PLAYING IN A ONE-KID BAND

SEAT YOUR TODDLER on your lap or on the floor in front of you for this favourite chant with silly sound effects. Create a slow beat by alternately slapping your hands on the floor and then clapping them together. Encourage your child to clap with you once you begin the chant. Repeat the chant's first two lines before you make a new motion and sound. When your toddler attempts to control his body to make a specific type of sound—such as stomping his feet or clicking his teeth—he improves both his language and motor skills.

Hey Mr. Knickerbocker, boppity, bop!
pat your hands flat on the floor once, clap, then repeat

I like the way you boppity, bop!
continue alternately patting and clapping to establish a beat

Listen to the sound we make with our hands.
rub palms to make a chafing sound

Listen to the sound we make with our feet.
stomp feet loudly on floor to the beat

Listen to the sound we make with our knees.
tap fingers softly on knees to the beat

Listen to the sound we make with our teeth.
click teeth together

Continue with other body parts.

✓ **Fine Motor Skills**

✓ **Gross Motor Skills**

✓ **Listening Skills**

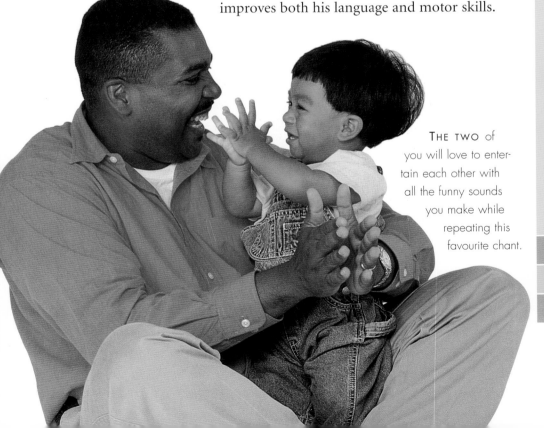

THE TWO of you will love to entertain each other with all the funny sounds you make while repeating this favourite chant.

61

PAPER-BAG BLOCKS

STACKING BIG BLOCKS

SKILLSPOTLIGHT

Children enhance *their fine motor skills and their ability to discriminate among shapes and sizes when they explore and play with blocks. Most kids also love to practise stacking the blocks—then knocking them down, of course. That provides a good lesson in balance, as well as in cause and effect. And if your child builds a little fort or cave, having a private space that's just his size can bolster his emerging sense of identity.*

Cause & Effect	✔
Fine Motor Skills	✔
Problem Solving	✔
Size & Shape Discrimination	✔
Spatial Awareness	✔

AT THIS AGE, his hands may be too small to skillfully manoeuvre heavy wooden blocks. But you can make large, lightweight blocks from paper bags and milk cartons that are both easy to handle and soft on impact.

• To make large blocks, fill a paper bag to the brim with crumpled newspaper. Fold and tape the sides of the open end as if you were wrapping a present. Help your child decorate the oversize blocks using non-permanent markers, crayons, wrapping paper, or stickers.

• For smaller blocks, thoroughly rinse and dry empty milk cartons. Open the tops and vertically cut through the corner creases to create flaps. Tape the flaps shut and cover the cartons with coloured paper or even sticky-back plastic with a brick motif (to create a "brick" house).

• Now let your junior architect begin to build. Encourage him to stack the blocks as high as he can or to use them to create little forts. A couch or a table and sheets can provide additional walls and a roof.

• Also show him how to stack the small blocks on top of the big blocks to build a toddler-size tower. When it's time to disassemble the stack, take turns removing one block at a time, and count the blocks out loud as you remove them. Then create new structures with your little builder.

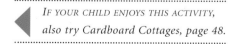

IF YOUR CHILD ENJOYS THIS ACTIVITY, also try Cardboard Cottages, page 48.

18 MONTHS
1½
AND UP

"Stack them high!"

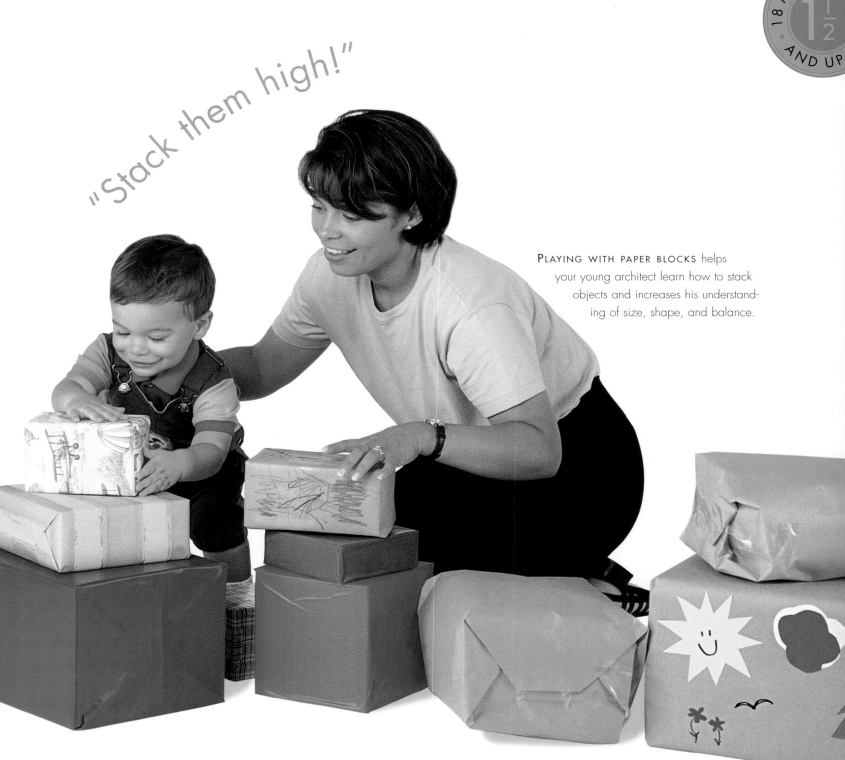

PLAYING WITH PAPER BLOCKS helps your young architect learn how to stack objects and increases his understanding of size, shape, and balance.

SIZE WISE

SORTING OUT NESTING CUPS

SKILL SPOTLIGHT

A nesting game *keeps toddler minds and hands busy as they learn to recognize differences in size. It also helps children learn to problem-solve ("How do I get these to all fit together?") and enhances eye-hand coordination and fine motor skills. The give-and-take between parent and child is important, too: your toddler is learning to listen and let you show her how to do things.*

Eye-Hand Coordination	✔
Fine Motor Skills	✔
Problem Solving	✔
Size & Shape Discrimination	✔

YOUNG TODDLERS derive endless pleasure from taking objects out of a container and then trying to put them back again. Increase the complexity and fun of this type of activity by introducing your child to nesting objects, which require her to fit things together in a particular order.

• You can buy nesting containers at toy stores. Or use measuring spoons, mixing bowls, or cardboard boxes of different sizes for the same effect.

• Some toddlers do not yet have the manual dexterity to get the objects to nest or to pull them apart again. Start out slowly by introducing your child to this activity with only two or three nesting cups that vary dramatically in size. Demonstrate how the items fit within each other. You may need to show her several times, but eventually she'll be able to help you; then she'll figure out how to nest the objects on her own.

• Gradually add to the number of nesting objects once she has mastered fitting the first few cups or bowls together.

IF THE BOWL FITS.... Teach your toddler some important lessons about size differences while satisfying her curiosity about your shiny kitchenware.

18 MONTHS 1½ AND UP

RESEARCH REPORT

A toddler's ability to sift through a jumble of cups and bowls and sort them into piles by size or shape demonstrates the dawning of logical reasoning. As exciting as it is to see a child master the simple but important concepts of same and different, it's obviously still a long journey to the type of sophisticated thinking associated with higher forms of logic. Jonas Langer, a psychologist at the University of California, found that a child's logical powers make a big jump in complexity between the ages of four and eight, but she isn't able to truly comprehend notions of abstract symbolism until she reaches age eleven or so.

65

HIDE YOUR EYES

SINGING THE PEEKABOO GAME

 to the *tune* of **"The Farmer in the Den"**

**Can you hide your eyes,
can you hide your eyes?
Yes you can, you surely can,
you can hide your eyes.**
cover your eyes with your hands

**Can you hide your nose,
can you hide your nose?
Yes you can, you surely can,
you can hide your nose.**
cover your nose with your hands

**Can you hide your feet,
can you hide your feet?
Yes you can, you surely can,
you can hide your feet.**
cover your feet with your hands

*Continue with chin, knees, toes,
elbows, ears, and so on.*

Body Awareness	✔
Creative Movement	✔
Language Development	✔

THIS SINGALONG takes a toddler favourite—the peekaboo game—and applies it to several parts of your child's body. In turn, this helps her learn the words for many of her body parts as well as how to sing along with others.

• Kick off the "Can You Hide Your Eyes?" song with the names of some easy body parts, such as eyes, nose, feet, and toes. Then graduate to less familiar words, like elbows, knees, chin, and neck.

• Make a few "mistakes" once in a while to see if she catches them—cover your knees when you say "toes," for instance, or cover her knees instead of yours. She'll be amused by these silly contradictions.

YOUR CHILD GETS TO PLAY peekaboo while singing when you add these new lyrics to an old, familiar tune.

SHAKE IT UP, BABY!

EXPERIMENTING WITH SOUND

INTRODUCE YOUR curious toddler to new sounds and rhythms by supplying her with child-size maracas or other percussion instruments (available in most toy stores). Or create your own little musicmakers by filling a few small plastic bottles with rice, dried beans, or pennies. (Close the lids tightly and seal them with packaging tape to avoid any accidents.) Begin by shaking each instrument or bottle, then pass it to your toddler, commenting on the unique sound it makes. Play a selection of familiar songs with different tempos and encourage her to make music and move her body to the beat.

A FEW HANDMADE instruments and a good song are all your toddler needs to let the rhythm move her.

SKILLSPOTLIGHT

Playing with musicmakers *stimulates auditory reflexes and nurtures a child's innate sense of rhythm, both of which are fundamental to language development. Identifying various kinds of sounds helps train the ear to recognize pitch and volume, while dancing and shaking or playing the instruments will encourage creative expression. If you make your own maracas, provide your child with additional tactile stimulation by allowing her to feel the rice, beans, and pennies before you put them in the bottles (but make sure she doesn't try to eat them).*

✔ **Creative Movement**

✔ **Listening Skills**

✔ **Rhythm Exploration**

✔ **Sensory Exploration**

67

SAND SKILLS

MAKING DESIGNS IN THE DIRT

SKILLSPOTLIGHT

Sand is wonderful *for artistic explorations because it allows a toddler to safely wallow in the medium from head to toe. Grasping and releasing the sand and using tools to manipulate it also exercise his fine motor skills and stimulate his sense of touch.*

Creative Expression	✔
Fine Motor Skills	✔
Tactile Stimulation	✔

If your child enjoys this activity, also try Nature Art, page 84. ▶

ZEN MASTERS DO IT. Bulldozers do it. And toddlers can do it, too. Whether you're at the beach, on a playground, or in a garden sandbox, making designs in the sand is absorbing, creative, and entertaining. It also provides a great way to combine artistic endeavours with healthy outdoor play.

• Gather a variety of tot-size tools, including sand toys (plastic buckets, shovels, and molds), kitchen utensils (spatulas, wooden spoons, and plastic containers), and garden tools (watering cans and miniature rakes).

• Pour water over the sand to make a more pliable palette.

• Show your child how to use the tools to make designs. He can draw a rake through the sand, for instance, to create straight or wavy rows of lines. Or press a cake tin into the sand to make a big circle. Use empty yoghurt containers and wet sand to add towers and turrets.

• Show your toddler how he can erase his creations by simply running his hands over the sand or by dumping a bucket of water on top of his mini masterpieces. Then let him wipe out and re-create his sand structures and patterns as many times as he likes.

MOST TODDLERS ARE THRILLED to play in a pile of sand; you can add to their fun by showing them how to make designs with sand toys and everyday kitchen tools.

PHOTO FUN

PUTTING NAMES TO FACES

Your toddler picks up *the rules of grammar by hearing your speech patterns. But she can't learn who Cousin Bill is or what an ostrich looks like just by listening. She needs a picture to put a face to a name. This activity aids in expanding her vocabulary, which in turn helps her organize and share her memories.*

MAKING YOUR OWN

Tape or glue photos to playing cards or index cards. For extra protection from enthusiastic little hands, laminate the cards at a local copy or framing shop. To hang, use tape or large magnets; avoid drawing pins and small magnets.

Language Development	✔
Visual Discrimination	✔
Visual Memory	✔

IT MAY SEEM like your toddler has nothing but a Be Here Now (or Give It to Me Now) perspective on life. But she's been able to store and retrieve memories since she was about six months old. Now she's driven to remember and practise saying the names of people and objects around her. This flash-card activity is a means of memorizing while having some fun.

• Tape or glue photos of family members and friends to index cards (this will enable your child to pick them up more easily). Point to someone in a picture and say the person's name. Pretty soon she'll be calling out their names even before you do.

• Glue these photos to a piece of coloured paper and laminate it for a "personalized" place mat.

• From photos cut out of magazines, make cards depicting appealing things that aren't already in her daily life, such as an anteater, giraffe, or helicopter. Hang the cards at eye level (on the refrigerator, for example) and point them out to her often.

• Attach stories to the images so your toddler will have an easier time remembering them. You can say, "We made biscuits with Grandma, didn't we?" or, "Rob has a big dog at his house, doesn't he?" This helps her learn how to tell stories, and it shows her that people are interested in them. It also helps her mentally process familiar events.

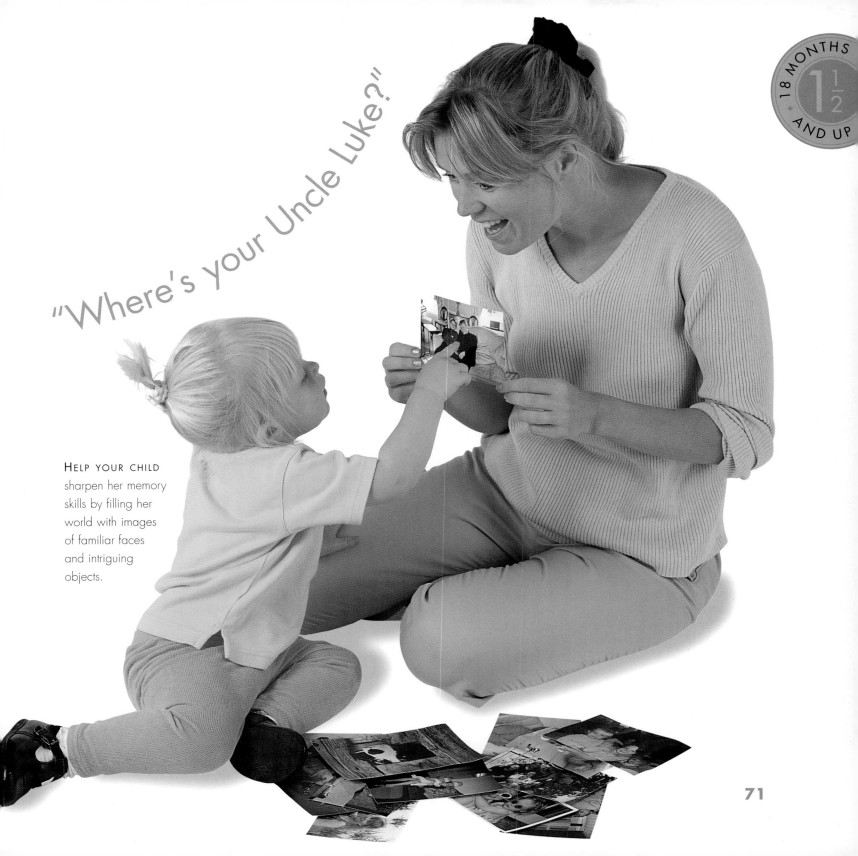

"Where's your Uncle Luke?"

HELP YOUR CHILD sharpen her memory skills by filling her world with images of familiar faces and intriguing objects.

THE MAGIC OF MUSIC

THE HUMAN passion for music is a universal trait, a gift parents from every culture naturally bestow on their children. We coo lullabies as babies drift off to sleep, clap as toddlers make their first wobbly forays onto the living-room dance floor, and play endless games of pat-a-cake with our youngsters. Which is a good thing: recent studies, such as the one outlining the much-publicized Mozart effect detailed on page 113, suggest that exposure to music has far-reaching intellectual benefits that go way beyond imparting a sense of melody and rhythm. Mark Tramo, a neuroscientist at Harvard Medical School, explains that the same mental pathways used to process music also seem to serve as conduits for language, maths, and abstract reasoning. "This means that exercising the brain through music strengthens other cognitive skills," Dr. Tramo concludes. The governor of the U.S. state of Georgia found this evidence so compelling he decided to send every baby born in Georgia home from the hospital with a recording of classical music. This book includes simple and enjoyable suggestions for filling your child's world with the sound of music, from the tape recorded parent-and-child duets on page 58 to the percussion games on page 88. Many of the activities link movement with music, which helps your toddler assimilate language and rhythm, develop coordination, and heighten body awareness. Complement these exercises by listening to a variety of music—while driving, eating, or doing housework or art projects, for example—and you'll further enhance her auditory senses and broaden her musical horizons. Don't feel you have to play classical music if that's not your favourite: introduce your child to the tunes you enjoy, and your pleasure can only make her more receptive to the value and power of all music. ■

TAMBOURINE TIME

MAKING MERRY MUSIC

THE TAMBOURINE IS MUSIC to your toddler's ears, arms, fingers, toes, and just about any other body part. Give him a tambourine and encourage him to shake it and tap it to the beat of his favourite songs—or to accompany you if you play an instrument. Move around as you play. Experiment with some tambourines of different sizes: how do the sounds of large and small ones compare? How does the sound change when you shake the tambourine hard, then shake it gently? The two of you can delight in each other's musical discoveries.

SKILLSPOTLIGHT

Simple musical instruments *offer toddlers a rich variety of activities that both stimulate and fine-tune auditory and tactile senses. As children play and listen, they begin to discriminate among different rhythms and types of sounds. And a tambourine, which can be either tapped or shaken, reinforces what toddlers are already discovering: that the world is full of unique and varied sounds —sounds they not only can recognize but can produce themselves.*

✔ **Eye-Hand Coordination**

✔ **Listening Skills**

✔ **Rhythm Exploration**

✔ **Social Skills**

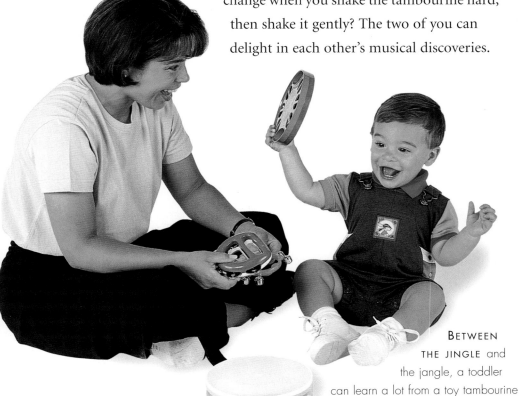

BETWEEN THE JINGLE and the jangle, a toddler can learn a lot from a toy tambourine.

73

CRAYON CREATIONS

ARTWORK ON A GRAND SCALE

SKILLSPOTLIGHT

Grasping and using *a crayon builds fine motor skills and eye-hand coordination. It also can help a child learn to identify colours. More important, letting him express himself by choosing his colours and scribbling in what-ever way he pleases allows him to give colour and shape to his bud-ding sense of identity. Discussing what the two of you are doing as you draw helps cement concepts in his memory and develop his communication skills.*

Concept Development	✔
Fine Motor Skills	✔
Social Skills	✔
Visual Memory	✔

EVEN CHILDREN as young as eighteen months are thrilled to put crayon and pen to paper. It can be hard for them to aim, however, and difficult to understand that the crayons or markers need to stay inside the paper's edges. Rather than fence him in with standard letter-size paper, let your child spread his artistic wings to create mural-size artwork.

• Clear a large area on the floor and tape down poster-size sheets of paper. Sit next to your toddler, hand him some non-permanent markers or crayons, and encourage him to scribble on the paper. You may have to show him how at first, but once he gets going, he won't want to stop.

• Talk about what you're doing as you draw. When he picks up a crayon, tell him what colour it is. Encourage him to use different colours and praise whatever marks he makes on the paper.

• With an older child, ask him to describe what he is drawing. If he's drawing a circle, for example, identify it and explain that it's round like a ball. Control your desire to help him make a perfect circle. It may only look like squiggly lines to you, but it's a masterpiece to him.

IF YOUR CHILD ENJOYS THIS ACTIVITY, also try Play With Clay, page 138. ▶

OVERSIZE CRAYONS and markers are easily gripped in the chubby fingers of your artist-in-the-making. Watch to see if he already has a favourite colour!

75

COUNT WITH ME

YOUR TODDLER is always happy to bounce on your knee and hear you sing, but songs and chants that emphasize counting add educational fun. While your child will love just to listen to you, she'll also begin to recognize numbers. Repetition reinforces the learning, so sing an encore or two.

FIVE LITTLE RAINDROPS

Five little raindrops falling from a cloud,
wiggle fingers on one hand downward
the first one said,
   "My, the thunder's loud."
   hold up one finger; cover ears

   The second one said,
   "It's so cold tonight."
   hold up two fingers; shiver and hug body

The third one said,
"Oh, the lightning's so bright."
hold up three fingers; cover eyes

The fourth one said,
"Listen to the wind blow."
hold up four fingers; cup hand at ear

The fifth one said,
"Look, I'm turning into snow."
hold up five fingers; float fingers down

So down they tumbled through the cold winter's night,
roll arms downward in front of body
and turned all the earth to a frosty, snowy white.

COUNTING RAINDROPS, caterpillars, and crayons is a fun way to introduce your child to the concept of numbers.

THE CATERPILLAR

One little caterpillar crawled on my shoe.
wiggle finger like a worm on a shoe

Along came another and then there were two.
show two fingers

Two little caterpillars crawled on my knee.
wiggle two fingers on knee

Along came another and then there were three.
show three fingers

Three little caterpillars crawled on the floor.
walk three fingers across the floor

Along came another and then there were four.
show four fingers

Four little caterpillars all crawled away.
walk four fingers across the floor

They will all turn into butterflies one fine day!
flap your arms like a butterfly

TEN LITTLE CRAYONS

 to the *tune* of **"Ten Little Indians"**

**One little, two little, three little crayons,
four little, five little, six little crayons,
seven little, eight little, nine little crayons,
ten little crayons in a box.**
hold up one finger for each crayon as you count them

Take out a red one and draw a big circle.
draw a circle with your finger

Take out a blue one and draw a straight line.
draw a straight line

Take out a yellow one and draw a little triangle.
draw a triangle

Then put them back in the box!
pretend to replace them in the crayon box

"WHERE'S DADDY? Oh! There he is!" A rousing game of hide-and-seek stimulates your toddler's curiosity while easing his separation anxieties.

HIDE-AND-SEEK

18 MONTHS 1½ AND UP

A FOLLOW-THE-VOICE GAME

THEY START WITH PEEKABOO when they're babies; later they'll startle you by shrieking "Boo!" as you turn the corner. In between, there's this sweet game of hide-and-seek designed just for a toddler.

• When your child's attention isn't focused directly on you, find a nearby tree, chair, or wall that you can hide behind. Call out to your toddler: "I'm hiding, try to find me!" As he searches, urge him closer with your voice. Soon he'll learn to follow the sound of your voice until he finds your hand, leg, shoulder, and, finally, your beloved face. Give him a congratulatory hug and play the game again.

• Teach him to hide so you can seek him out. He'll mostly hide his head, forgetting that you can see his little legs sticking out from behind the bed or his fingers clutching the blanket. But make a big show of pretending you don't see him. Then act surprised when you happen to find him.

SKILLSPOTLIGHT

Following the direction *of a sound, such as Daddy's voice, teaches children to listen carefully. And as your child learns that the part of you that's sticking out— whether it's your shoulder or your feet—is attached to the rest of you, he'll strengthen his visual memory.*

✔	**Concept Development**
✔	**Listening Skills**
✔	**Social Skills**
✔	**Visual Discrimination**
✔	**Visual Memory**

IF YOUR CHILD ENJOYS THIS ACTIVITY, also try Mystery Sounds, page 141. ▶

79

CEREAL CHALLENGE

GETTING TO THE CONTENTS

SKILLSPOTLIGHT

This is a deceptively simple *activity that promotes problem-solving techniques and exemplifies the concepts behind in and out and the principle of cause and effect. Once your child has mastered this challenge, raise the stakes with this visual memory game: take three plastic yoghurt or margarine containers and hide a cereal bit in one of them. Mix them up, then urge her to find the one with the cereal (also see Magic Cups, page 131).*

Cause & Effect	✔
Concept Development	✔
Fine Motor Skills	✔
Problem Solving	✔

FIND A CLEAN, unbreakable small-mouthed bottle (a plastic baby bottle or water bottle works well) and drop some of your toddler's favourite breakfast cereal or snack into it. Show your toddler the cereal in the open bottle and ask her to get it out. Allow her to experiment, but if she becomes overly frustrated, demonstrate how to tip the bottle over. Increase the challenge by lightly screwing on the top or asking her to drop the cereal back into the bottle. To further fine-tune her motor skills, try this with a variety of containers that have different types of lids.

BOTTOMS UP! There's nothing like a snack to motivate your budding genius—just watch how quickly she catches on.

80

18 MONTHS 1½ AND UP

SHAPE TO FIT

PUZZLING OUT A SOLUTION

SKILLSPOTLIGHT

WHICH SHAPES GO WHERE? Toddlers love a mystery, and this is one they can solve with some help from you. Use a shape-sorter toy or cut out three or four simple shapes on the top and sides of some sturdy cardboard boxes. (Make sure the shapes are about the same size so the triangle won't fit into the hole for the circle, for instance.) Ask your toddler to drop the shapes into the matching holes. Demonstrate the activity to get your child started, then let your young detective work on this visual mystery at her own pace.

MATCHING UP SHAPES teaches more than geometry; a child also learns how to "puzzle out" solutions to challenges of all kinds.

The ability to classify and discriminate among sizes and shapes is a fundamental skill that not only helps toddlers make sense of the world but prepares them for activities they'll encounter in play groups and preschool. Sorting, grasping, and fitting shapes also promotes the development of fine motor skills and eye-hand coordination, which will in turn aid toddlers as they practise using forks and spoons, manipulating toys, and colouring. It may take some time before your child is able to easily discriminate among shapes, but most children this age enjoy practising.

✔ **Classifying Skills**

✔ **Eye-Hand Coordination**

✔ **Fine Motor Skills**

✔ **Size & Shape Discrimination**

81

POINT OUT THE PARTS

TALKING ABOUT THE BODY

SKILL SPOTLIGHT

Identifying and repeating *the names of specific body parts plays a role in language development; not only is your child learning to match your real nose to the word "nose," she's also feeling what a nose is by touching it or sniffing with it. The resulting physical sensations increase her awareness of her body and her body parts.*

Body Awareness	✔
Concept Development	✔
Language Development	✔
Listening Skills	✔

LABELLING BODY PARTS is an important first step in your child's sense of herself as a separate person. This simple activity aids the process of self-discovery, which begins at the end of the first year of life and blossoms in the second. This game also sharpens your toddler's verbal skills and memory, and increases her awareness of her body.

● To start this activity, sit facing your child and touch her nose. Then take her finger in your hand and guide it to your nose. Say "nose" several times as you tap her finger on your nose. Then ask her to point to her own nose. Continue with other body parts, such as head, arm, leg, and foot. It may take her a while to distinguish between "Mummy's nose" and "baby's nose"—that's natural. But eventually this will become a favourite game of hers and one that gives her a sense of accomplishment.

● If she has the verbal skills to say some of the names of the body parts, ask her to repeat them as you point to them. Or initiate a movement game that shows her how to shake her head, stomp her foot, sniff through her nose, and wiggle her tiny toes.

◄ IF YOUR CHILD ENJOYS THIS ACTIVITY, also try Hide Your Eyes, page 66.

KNOWING THE DIFFERENCE between Mummy's hair and her own mouth is a major milestone for a proud pointer. Next, talk about how her hands are small and yours are big.

"Look at this tiny leaf."

PRESSING GARDEN TREASURES
between sticky-back plastic is a
creative way to cultivate a love
of the outdoors.

84

NATURE ART

CREATING A NATURAL COLLAGE

TODDLERS LOVE THE OUTDOORS, love to collect things, and love to dabble in the arts—as you've no doubt noticed with your child's oatmeal finger paintings at breakfast time or perhaps her crayon murals. Nurture this trio of passions by helping your toddler create a collage of natural elements.

• Take her on a walk in your garden, a park, or the woods and collect small leaves, flowers, grass, sticks, feathers, and whatever else she finds that appeals to her (and is safe to handle).

• Use the outing as a time to expose your child to some new words and concepts by talking about what you find ("See this feather? That's from a magpie." "Look, the flowers are turned toward the sun.").

• Once you're home, place a piece of clear sticky-back plastic, sticky side up, on top of a baking sheet with a rim. Tape the corners of the sticky plastic to the baking sheet to keep it from adhering to your hands.

• Help your child arrange her outdoor treasures on the baking sheet.

• Place another piece of clear sticky-back plastic, sticky side down, over the first one to help preserve your toddler's work of art.

• Hang the collage in a window, on the refrigerator, even in your child's room . . . anywhere she can proudly showcase her creation.

IF YOUR CHILD ENJOYS THIS ACTIVITY, also try Tree Talk, page 100. ▶

SKILLSPOTLIGHT

Letting your child choose *her own objects (a red flower versus a yellow one, for instance) and arrange them herself helps her identify and express her personal preferences. Talking to her about nature as you explore the outdoors encourages her to notice and describe the world. And the task of applying objects to paper—or a sheet of sticky-back plastic—helps enhance her fine motor skills.*

✔	**Creative Expression**
✔	**Eye-Hand Coordination**
✔	**Fine Motor Skills**
✔	**Language Development**

WATER THE PLANTS

A MUSICAL MIME

 to the *tune* of **"The Mulberry Bush"**

This is the way we water the plants,
put one hand on hip and bend the other like a curved spout
**water the plants,
water the plants.**

**This is the way we water the plants
whenever they get dry.**

We water the plants so they will grow,
crouch down on the floor, then slowly stand up
**they will grow,
they will grow.**

**We water the plants so they will grow
way up to the sky.**
raise your hands skyward

Balance	✓
Coordination	✓

THIS GARDENING SONG will teach your tyke a fundamental lesson about nature: that plants need water to grow! Show your child how to tip way over as he "pours" the water from his "spout." That's good balance practice. If he likes rowdier play, you may want to pick him up and tip him over instead. Reinforce the gardening lesson by asking him to help you water real plants, either inside or outside. He'll enjoy participating in your chores (see Copycat, page 178) and nurturing living things.

TWISTING LIKE A SPOUT gives your little one a handle on what makes gardens grow.

SURPRISE!

18 MONTHS 1½ AND UP

UNWRAPPING TOY TREASURES

FOR TODDLERS, the wrapping on a present is at least as fun as the gift itself. They love the brightly coloured paper, the noise it makes when they crinkle it, and the challenge of discovering what's inside. Your child can enjoy this activity any day of the year if you gather several of his favourite toys and wrap them loosely in colourful paper (no tape) while he watches.

• Show him one package at a time, asking, "What's inside the paper?" Let him remove the wrapping—but lend a helping hand if he gets frustrated. Crumple up the paper and comment on the sound it makes and how it feels.

SKILLSPOTLIGHT

Unwrapping an object *requires problem solving and nimble fingers. Playing with different patterns and textures stimulates a child's visual, tactile, and auditory senses, especially when the paper crinkles or pops as it's handled.*

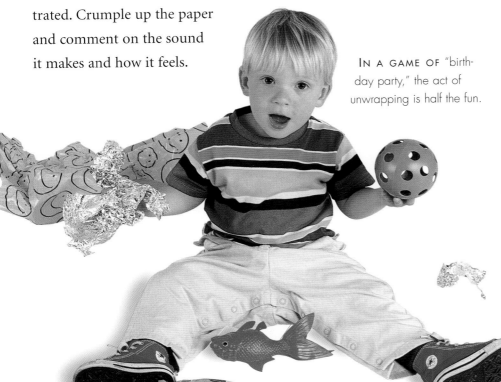

IN A GAME OF "birthday party," the act of unwrapping is half the fun.

✔	**Coordination**
✔	**Problem Solving**
✔	**Sensory Exploration**
✔	**Tactile Discrimination**

87

RHYTHM TIME

FUN WITH A DRUM

SKILLSPOTLIGHT

Your child is born *with an innate sense of rhythm. But learning to pound out a beat—especially while practising with you—lets her see how it fits into music, dance, and other rhythmic activities. Drumming also enhances her eye-hand coordination, and learning to vary the pace and volume fine-tunes her muscle control.*

Cause & Effect	✔
Creative Expression	✔
Listening Skills	✔
Rhythm Exploration	✔

MAKING YOUR OWN

Creating a drum is as simple as turning over a saucepan or wooden bowl. Try metal, plastic, and wooden spoons for varying sound effects; use different-size containers to create varying pitches (the smaller they are, the higher the pitch).

YOUR CHILD ALREADY KNOWS how to make plenty of noise by banging her spoon on the table, clapping her hands, and pounding on the door she wants opened. You can direct this energy toward more musical pursuits—as well as encourage her sense of rhythm— by showing her how to bang out a beat with a drum.

• Buy a drum and mallet (or make your own). Sit down with your child and show her how to hit the drum with either a mallet or her hand. Demonstrate how to hit the drum softly, then loudly. Vary the pace of the drumming so she experiences fast as well as slow beats.

• Put on some lively music and demonstrate how to drum to the beat. Don't expect her to follow the music exactly—that will come when she's older. Sway back and forth, tap your foot, clap your hands, and toss your head from side to side to show her other ways of expressing rhythm. Or get your own drum and pound out a noisy duet.

◀ *IF YOUR CHILD ENJOYS THIS ACTIVITY, also try Shake It Up, Baby!, page 67.*

SHOW YOUR LITTLE DRUMMER GIRL
the different sounds she can make, then
let her march to her own beat.

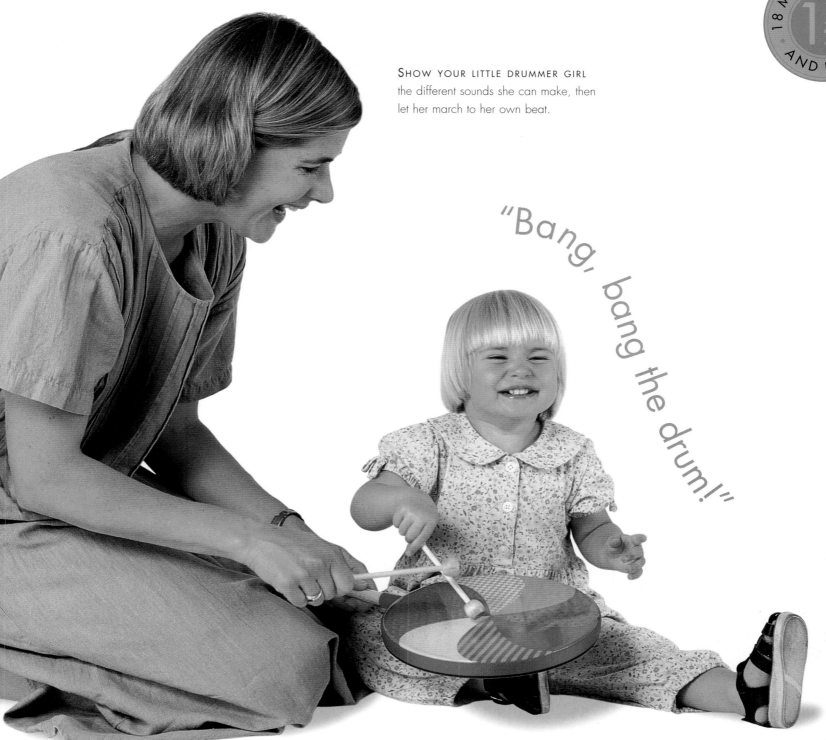

"Bang, bang the drum!"

TODDLER PARADE

MAKING A SPECIAL DAY WITH EVERYDAY TOYS

SKILL SPOTLIGHT

This is the very beginning *of fantasy play: she's pretending to be a member of the parade and she's mentally converting her toys (and her parent) into appropriate props. Walking (or even marching) to music can help her learn rhythm. And she'll develop new levels of coordination by figuring out how to pull her pretend-parade behind her.*

Creative Expression	✔
Fine Motor Skills	✔
Gross Motor Skills	✔

EVERYONE LOVES A PARADE— but you don't have to wait for a bank holiday or struggle with crowds to let your toddler participate in one. Instead, create a pint-size parade in your own home, complete with music and marchers (albeit fuzzy ones). Make your child the star of the parade.

• Help her collect her wheeled toys in the "staging grounds" (for example, your living room). Tie the toys together with short lengths of string so she can pull the makeshift contraption behind her. If you have a toy cart, prop stuffed animals inside to serve as famous folk. To get really fancy, decorate the "floats" with streamers and ribbons. You could even make confetti!

NOTHING CAN RAIN on their personal parade when they have their rolling elephants, horses, and lion marching right along behind them.

• When your toddler gets a little older, play lively marching music, outfit yourself with a drum (a spoon and a pot will do) or a fake baton, and start parading around with your child in tow. She probably won't be able to march and pull her toys at the same time, so pull the floats for her while she practises stepping high and swinging her little arms.

RESEARCH REPORT

In studies conducted *in the United States and Britain, psychologists Anthony Pellegrini and Peter K. Smith showed that children instinctively seem to understand the importance of play and freedom of movement. When their free play was restricted for a period of time, the "deprivation led to increased levels of play when opportunities for play were resumed," the psychologists concluded. In other words, when finally let loose, the kids tried to make up for lost playtime.*

IF YOUR CHILD ENJOYS THIS ACTIVITY, also try Band on the Run, page 44.

PLAYING WITH SIBLINGS

WHEN PLAYING one-on-one with a toddler, you can easily adapt to your child's needs and desires. But when a sibling is introduced into the group, the dynamics change dramatically, calling for a parent to exercise a bit more imagination and diplomacy.

Several factors complicate the situation: toddlers aren't always keen on sharing their parents' attention, even with a beloved brother or sister. If there's more than a two-year gap in ages, just finding an activity that suits both children can be a challenge. Then there are different play styles to consider: one child may be the quiet type who prefers to play alone with blocks, while his dynamo of a sister likes nothing more than to help him build block towers—before knocking them down. No wonder a session of family fun can leave you feeling more like a referee in a particularly fierce World Wrestling Federation match than a play partner.

Still, there are many ways to ensure smoother, more enjoyable play sessions. Taking into account the children's ages and personalities, devise activities that will be fun for both and accommodate different play styles. Art projects such as drawing with pavement chalk or painting, for instance, can be enjoyed by toddlers and young school-age children alike. Going to a playground outfitted with a variety of equipment allows children to play together for a while, and then pursue individual interests. And don't forget to stock up on duplicate toys and supplies when possible; having two sets of watercolours and two rainbow-coloured balls has saved many a parent from sibling meltdown. It's also important to dole out attention in fairly equal measures. While it's natural to pay more attention to the younger child, as she might need more help, remember to offer words of praise or encouragement to the older sibling. ■

BABY BASKETBALL

18 MONTHS 1½ AND UP

SLAM-DUNKING A FAVOURITE GAME

GATHER A FEW medium-size balls and place them in a large container such as a laundry basket, cardboard box, or plastic bowl. Show your child how to empty the balls onto the floor, then demonstrate how to drop the balls one by one into the basket. Initially, your toddler may enjoy simply putting the balls in the basket and taking them back out. When he's ready, have him stand back and try throwing the balls into the basket. Increase the challenge by placing a few containers around the room, then urge your athlete to aim towards a different one each time.

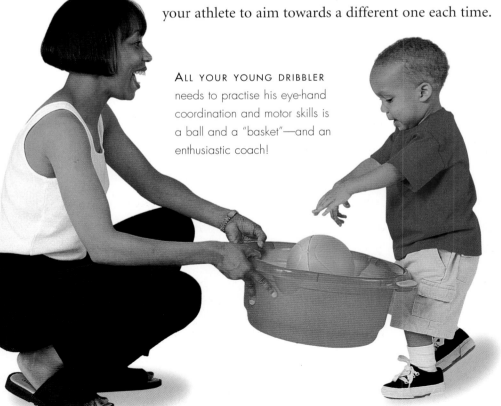

ALL YOUR YOUNG DRIBBLER needs to practise his eye-hand coordination and motor skills is a ball and a "basket"—and an enthusiastic coach!

SKILL SPOTLIGHT

When your child practises aiming, he improves his eye-hand coordination and gross motor skills. And if you count the balls out loud as your toddler throws them into the containers you'll help lay the foundation for understanding numbers. Whether your child is tossing the ball into a basket or at you, actively participate by gently throwing it back to him and encourage him to take another (more difficult) fundamental step: learning to catch.

✔	**Eye-Hand Coordination**
✔	**Gross Motor Skills**
✔	**Social Skills**

93

THE GRAND OLD DUKE OF YORK

A CLASSIC SONG AND MIME

SKILL SPOTLIGHT

Your toddler *is beginning to form a clearer sense of himself as an object in space. This song game—while fun to play with a parent—helps him learn the meanings of spatial words, such as up, down, and over. And while your child may not be quite old enough to tell right from left, he'll get the idea, at least, that those words refer to something other than straight ahead.*

Concept Development	✔
Language Development	✔
Spatial Awareness	✔

IF YOUR CHILD ENJOYS THIS ACTIVITY, also try The Choo-Choo Train, page 98. ▶

94

UNDERSTANDING THE CONCEPTS of space and movement proceeds slowly but surely in the toddler years. If your child loved lap songs as a baby, he'll get a big kick out of this more advanced version, which teaches him just some of the ways he can move about in the world.

• As with all song games, enunciating the sounds clearly and emphasizing the corresponding movements help teach your toddler the meaning of the most important words. Those emphases also create a song with more drama and vigour, which makes it more exciting for the two of you.

• As your toddler gets older, he can sing this song standing on the floor instead of sitting on your knees. Try marching during the first stanza, then stretching up and crouching down in the second stanza. With the third stanza, have him drop to the floor and lie on his back, then gently push his legs left, right, and up in the air.

THIS FUN TUNE—bolstered by Mummy's bouncy movements—helps your little duke learn about moving up and down.

The Grand Old Duke of York, he had ten thousand men,
bounce child on your knees, facing outward
he marched them up to the top of the hill,
march your legs upward with child still on knees
and he marched them down again.
march your legs downward with child still on knees

And when you're up, you're up.
raise both legs
And when you're down, you're down.
drop both legs
And when you're only halfway up,
raise both legs halfway up and pause
you're neither up nor down.
move legs up and down quickly

He rolled them over left,
lean to the left
he rolled them over right,
lean to the right
he rolled them over upside down,
lie backward with child lying on top of you
oh, what a funny sight!
return to original position

TUBE TRICKS

WHERE DOES THE BALL GO?

SKILL SPOTLIGHT

At eighteen months *she's still fascinated by balls and disappearing acts, and she still thrills to repetition. But it's not all fun and games here. Dropping balls into a tube and then catching (or chasing) them exercises her fine motor skills as well as eye-hand coordination. Taking turns at either end of the tube promotes sharing. And fitting different-size balls into the tube helps her sort shapes in her mind.*

MAKING YOUR OWN

You can find tubes of all sizes at art supply shops, poster shops, newsagents, framing shops, and the post office. Any soft balls that fit in the tube will work: tennis balls, squash balls, or balls made of cloth, soft rubber, or foam.

Cause & Effect	✔
Fine Motor Skills	✔
Size & Shape Discrimination	✔

I N ONE END . . . out the other—it seems simple to us, but to a toddler it's like playing hide-and-seek with a ball, which is sure to puzzle and thrill her. Even when she's mastered the mystery ("Where did the ball go? Oh! There it is!"), she'll want to play this game over and over again.

• Start with a wide plastic or cardboard tube and a supply of tennis, squash, or other soft balls. Put the balls in one end of the tube, tilt the tube so they roll down inside it, and have her retrieve them from the other end. Repeat several times and then switch places.

• Increase the complexity by using balls of different sizes. Which ones fit in the tube? Which ones don't? Be sure to choose balls that are at least 4.5 cm (1¾ inches) in diameter so they're not a choking hazard.

• You can turn this activity into a coordination exercise by asking her to catch a ball as it's falling out of the tube. You stand up, she waits at the bottom end of the tube, and as the ball pops out, she tries to grab it. The smaller the ball, the greater the challenge.

◀ *IF YOUR CHILD ENJOYS THIS ACTIVITY, also try Baby Basketball, page 93.*

18 MONTHS
1 1/2
AND UP

A CLEAR TUBE lets her watch the blue balls roll all the way from top to bottom; an opaque tube will add an element of surprise to the game.

18 MONTHS 1½ AND UP

THE CHOO-CHOO TRAIN

AN EXCURSION IN RHYME

Sit facing your child and hold both of her hands.

Here comes the choo-choo train coming down the track. First it's going forward, then it's going back.
pull one hand toward you while pushing the other toward your child; continue to alternate

Now the bell is ringing: ding, ding, ding!
ring imaginary bell

Now the whistle blows: whoo, whoo, whoo!
pull imaginary whistle cord

What a lot of noise it makes
cover both of your ears
everywhere it goes!

| Language Development | ✔ |
| Rhythm Exploration | ✔ |

TODDLERS DON'T NEED a melody to sense rhythm: they can feel "beats" with simple chants. When you add appealing rhymes, fun movements, an ever-friendly train theme, and an enthusiastic parent, you've got an activity that will keep your little one chugging merrily along.

• While you chant "Here Comes the Choo-Choo Train," play up the rhythm so your toddler can hear it and mimic it with her body. Try to ham up the movements, too. Emphasizing the gestures will help your eager engineer understand the meaning of the accompanying words.

THIS CHANTING game teaches your little conductor to feel a beat, "blow" a whistle, and understand the basics of moving forward and backward.

18 MONTHS
1½
AND UP

TANTALIZING TEXTURES

A BOOK OF SENSATIONS

HE'S ALREADY DETERMINED to get his hands on everything in (and out of) sight, including dollops of jam, dead insects, and months-old cereal bits. Let his fingers experience the world safely by introducing him to a book filled with tactile adventures. You can buy the book or make your own.

• To make a texture book, collect a variety of materials, such as cloth, hessian, foil, wax paper, and bubble wrap. Glue a large square of each material onto cardboard or coloured paper. Then tie or tape the sheets together.

• When you explore the book with your toddler, describe the different sensations you both are feeling.

SKILLSPOTLIGHT

A texture book *lets your toddler discover a variety of different materials and helps him learn concepts such as rough, smooth, bumpy, and even squishy. The book can also give your child the chance to express his preferences: Does he like the scratchy feel of hessian? Or does he prefer the crinkliness of the foil?*

✔ **Language Development**

✔ **Tactile Discrimination**

✔ **Tactile Stimulation**

BOOK PAGES made of unusual textures, such as fine sandpaper or fake fur, let your child explore the world from the safety of your lap.

99

RESEARCH REPORT

If your child seems particularly adept at telling oak leaves from maple and has no trouble telling a grasshopper from a cricket, he might be exhibiting what renowned Harvard psychologist Howard Gardner calls "naturalist intelligence." Gardner, who previously identified seven other kinds of intelligences (such as linguistic and logical-mathematical), defines naturalist intelligence as the ability to recognize and classify flora and fauna. "Someone with a high degree of this intelligence," he says, "is comfortable in the world of organisms and may well possess the talent of caring for, taming, or interacting subtly with a variety of living creatures."

TREE TALK

WALKING ON THE WILD SIDE

WHETHER YOU LIVE in a city, a suburb, or the country, your toddler is probably already drawn to all things treelike. You can encourage this natural affinity by spending time in leafy neighbourhoods, parks, or forests and helping him discover the tremendous beauty of botanical life.

• Show him the leaves, trunks, roots, and branches. Encourage him to explore the roughness of the bark, the smoothness of the leaves, and the gnarled contours of the roots. Also ask him to listen (for rustling leaves or birdcalls) and to smell (rich soil and fragrant blossoms, for instance).

• Look for creatures that inhabit the trees, including squirrels, birds, and insects. Point out their homes, such as the bird's nest.

• Explain the importance of respecting all forms of life, even the little creeping ones. To help him with this, pick up some of the harmless insects (caterpillars or ladybirds) and show them to him up close.

• When your toddler reaches age two or more, collect acorns, leaves, pinecones, and fallen pieces of bark to take home and make into a collage (see Nature Art, page 84) or a nature book.

• Name a few of the more common types of trees and explain how he can identify them. ("See the white bark on that one? That's a birch tree. But the tree with the green needles is a pine tree.")

SKILL SPOTLIGHT

Learning all about trees *and the animals that live in them is an important step toward understanding nature in its many forms. Discovering an interest in—rather than a fear of—creepy-crawly creatures provides an essential building block for the development of compassion and an early appreciation of the wonder of natural science.*

✔ **Language Development**
✔ **Sensory Exploration**
✔ **Visual Discrimination**

IF YOUR CHILD ENJOYS THIS ACTIVITY, also try Care for the Animals, page 128.

GIVING YOUR TODDLER a Daddy's-eye view of a tree's tender leaves helps him learn to appreciate nature.

MAGNET MAGIC

SKILLSPOTLIGHT

Grasping and moving *magnets helps build fine motor skills—the ones he'll need for drawing, completing puzzles, fastening little buttons, and, eventually, writing. Talking about these intriguing magnets helps him learn to distinguish among colours and sizes and contributes to the expansion of his vocabulary, while making a magnet "disappear" exercises his visual memory.*

Counting Concepts	✔
Fine Motor Skills	✔
Size & Shape Discrimination	✔
Visual Memory	✔

MAKING YOUR OWN

Create personalized magnets by gluing or taping photos of family members onto inexpensive, flat magnets. Or attach photos, drawings, or magazine pictures of your child's favourite animals. Photo shops carry magnetized photo frames, as well.

MANY CHILDREN display their manual dexterity by pulling magnets off the refrigerator—and then crowing delightedly over their finds. You can make magnets even more fun by using them for a variety of games that engage your child's eyes and memory, as well as his curious fingers.

• Gather several colourful magnets and place them on a metal baking sheet (note: magnets won't adhere to aluminium sheets). Use magnets with images of objects your toddler likes, such as animals, flowers, food, storybook characters, numbers, and vehicles. Always be sure to avoid magnets that are smaller than 4.5 cm (1¾ inches) in diameter because they pose a choking hazard. And make sure the magnet has a well-defined edge so your child can pick it up easily.

• Ask your toddler to take the magnets off the sheet—then ask him to put them back on. Talk to him about the colours, sizes, and characters he sees on the magnets. Encourage him to move them around to create his own design. With an older toddler, try removing a magnet from the sheet and asking him to guess which one is missing.

◀ *IF YOUR CHILD ENJOYS THIS ACTIVITY,*
also try Tantalizing Textures, page 99.

YOUR TODDLER IS FAR TOO YOUNG to understand magnetic attraction, but learning that certain objects adhere to a baking sheet is the very beginning of scientific discovery.

103

18 MONTHS
1½
AND UP

OPEN SHUT THEM!

A TICKLING RHYME

Open shut them,
open and close fists
open shut them,
give a little clap, clap, clap!
clap three times

Open shut them,
open and close fists
open shut them,
put them in your lap, lap, lap!
pat lap three times

Creep them, crawl them,
slowly creep them,
right up to your chin, chin, chin!
walk fingers from chest to chin,
tickling your child along the way

Open wide your little mouth,
touch lips with a finger
but do not let them in!
quickly run fingers down to lap,
tickling your child along the way

Creative Expression	✔
Fine Motor Skills	✔
Language Development	✔

TODDLERS HAVE A GREAT LOVE for their own little bodies—and the names of their own little body parts. They also enjoy tickle and surprise games. This rhyme gives your child a chance to show off her knowledge of her body and at the same time play a creepy-crawly tickle game.

• Start out by demonstrating the rhyme's gestures on yourself and see if she can follow along. If she seems confused, do the fingerplay on her instead—until she is ready to copy you.

YOUR CHILD will enjoy playing the creepy-crawly game with her fingers—especially when Mummy is an active participant.

BEACH-BALL CATCH

A TOSS-AND-CATCH BALL GAME

MOST TODDLERS are able to throw a ball before they can catch one. But they love trying to wrap their little arms around airborne balls, and with a healthy dose of patience and practice you can help your child learn the basics of catching. Start by rolling a ball to her and asking her to roll it back to you (see Pass the Ball, page 24). When she's ready to attempt catching, use a slightly deflated beach ball (it's easier for small hands to grasp).

* Kneel or sit a couple of feet apart and ask her to throw the beach ball to you. Demonstrate how to catch, then toss the ball to her and ask her to catch it. Once she accomplishes this (it will take a lot of practice), increase the distance between you, little by little.

YOUR CHILD will catch on more quickly if you show her how to grab the ball before you toss it her way.

SKILL SPOTLIGHT

Playing a game *of catch with a toddler is a fun and simple exercise in socialization that builds gross motor skills and eye-hand coordination. Successful catches demand quick reflexes and good spatial awareness, which may take a while for your toddler to achieve. By enthusiastically supporting your child in her attempts to catch, you are teaching her to appreciate being part of a game in a non-competitive way.*

✔	**Eye-Hand Coordination**
✔	**Gross Motor Skills**
✔	**Social Skills**

105

BALANCING ACT

STANDING TALL ON A BALANCE BEAM

SKILLSPOTLIGHT

Balance beams, *logs, and low walls present an irresistible challenge to curious young children. As she perfects her walk along the beam, her ability to balance increases, and she develops crucial eye-foot coordination—skills that will help her as she moves from walking to running, jumping, hopping, skipping, and—who knows?—maybe even perfecting a gymnastic dismount.*

Balance	✔
Eye-Foot Coordination	✔
Spatial Awareness	✔

IF YOUR CHILD ENJOYS THIS ACTIVITY, also try Footstep Fun, page 125. ▶

ATTEMPTING TO BALANCE on narrow walkways is a natural and universal activity for young children, so you probably won't have to do much to encourage your child to try. You can find beams low enough to walk on safely at gyms, parks, and playgrounds. Demonstrate how to walk across, then hold your child's hand as she tries to walk slowly on the beam.

• If your toddler is reluctant at first, place a toy at the other end of the beam and encourage your young gymnast to hold your hand and walk across to retrieve it. Be sure she practises this balancing act above a soft or cushioned surface.

SHE'LL BE SUREFOOTED in no time with her favourite coach by her side for support.

106

PUPPET PLAY

24 MONTHS
2
AND UP

AN OLD-FASHIONED STAGE SHOW

CHILDREN ADORE PUPPETS because they're toys that seem to magically come to life. They'll love them even more when you put on a live, slapstick show. You can buy some fancy puppets—or just use brightly coloured felt-tipped pens to draw a face on a sock or a bag. You can even tape ears or horns on your homemade puppet and glue "hair" made of yarn to its top.

• Make a stage by draping a blanket over the back of a chair or a safety gate—or position yourself behind a sofa. With one or two puppets, tell your child stories and sing songs. Use a different voice for each puppet.

• Ask your child questions with the puppets and encourage him to converse. Question him about his favourite foods, his special toys, or his mummy and daddy. And ask him to show the puppet his nose and toes—toddlers love to point these things out.

SKILL SPOTLIGHT

By the age of two, *your child is attributing all sorts of human traits to his toys; he considers them his best friends. By making puppet toys act more like humans, you stimulate his imagination. And by telling stories and conversing with him, you accelerate his back-and-forth conversational skills.*

✔	**Imagination**
✔	**Language Development**
✔	**Social Skills**

A BIG, FAT FROG and a polka-dotted duck can share some pretty funny stories with their little human friend.

107

TRAIN TRIPS

AN IMAGINARY LOCOMOTIVE

SKILLSPOTLIGHT

In this activity, *your little train driver enhances her upper body muscle coordination and learns to move with the rhythm of a chant. Puffing along as your pint-size passenger, she develops whole body coordination as well as balance—after all, it's hard to stay seated on Mummy when you're busy giggling like crazy. Role-playing also greases the gears of the imagination.*

Coordination	✔
Gross Motor Skills	✔
Imagination	✔
Social Skills	✔

YOU CAN HARNESS your child's abundant steam power by taking her on an imaginary train trip. Announce your destination ("First stop, Mummy's lap!"), pretend to pull the whistle ("Whoo whoo!"), then invite her to sit on your lap. As you chant "chug-a-chug-a-choo-choo," push her hands in a circle (like the rolling train wheels) or help her blow the whistle. Alternatively, you can both "chug" around the house ("Next stop, your bedroom!") with your child as the engine and you as the carriage.

• Pretend to navigate around curves by bending both of your bodies from side to side. Go through "tunnels" (don't forget to duck your heads!) and stop from time to time to let passengers off at the "station."

• Sing a favourite train song or chant (see The Choo-Choo Train, page 98) while you chug around the house together.

• To help a toddler appreciate trains and enjoy this activity even more, take her to a real train station—or even the underground—and show your young conductor what it's like to ride the rails.

IF YOUR CHILD ENJOYS THIS ACTIVITY, also try Drive the Fire Engine, page 134.

"Whoo whoo! All aboard!"

SHE'LL EXPAND her locomotor skills and blow off a good bit of steam in this vigorous lap game.

THE "NO" STAGE

ONE OF THE biggest shocks to new parents is the transformation of their easygoing, compliant infants into mercurial toddlers whose favourite word seems to be "no"—as in "no bananas," "no bath," and "no songs," even though they never seemed to mind these things before. As Dr. Benjamin Spock wrote in *Baby and Child Care,* "When you suggest something that doesn't appeal to them, they feel they must assert themselves. . . . Psychologists call it 'negativism.'" While admitting that this spell of negativism can test the resources of even the most patient parents, Spock also noted that this stage is an important signal that children are maturing into independent human beings who can think for themselves.

Being calm, cooperative, and reasonable with your toddler is one of the most effective ways to teach him to be a calm, cooperative, and reasonable person himself—but it will take time. Until he learns more self-control, you can expect temper tantrums when he doesn't get his way. It's best to ignore such behaviour—if possible—to convey that he can't get what he wants in this unseemly manner. In *Raising Good Children,* developmental psychologist Thomas Lickona advises parents to keep toddlers happily busy, offer diversions when they get restless, and allow lots of free play in safe settings. He also recommends counting, such as saying, "Let's see if you can get in your chair by the time I count to ten." Another strategy is to present a child with alternatives. If he insists on wearing weather-inappropriate clothes, you could pick out two other suitable outfits and say, "Which would you like to wear today?" Such manoeuvres might seem transparent to adults, but they are wonderfully effective in making a headstrong toddler feel a measure of the control and freedom he so desires. ■

PONY RIDES

24 MONTHS
2
AND UP

TAKING A LIVING-ROOM TROT

SHE'S FASCINATED by pictures of horses, but a wee bit wary of the real thing. Give her a leg up on balance skills by playing the pony part yourself. Get down on your hands and knees and let your child "ride" on your back or shoulders. Make sure she hangs on tight, and be ready to grab a leg if she starts sliding.

• If you want to add music to this activity, sing "Trot Little Pony" (see Silly Lap Songs on page 54 for the lyrics) or another of your toddler's favourite songs as you crawl around the room. To help her learn to adjust her balance, lower your upper body to the floor, raise it (not too high!), or wiggle from side to side.

GIDDYUP DADDY! You can start your little cowgirl's riding lessons early by doing some of the legwork in your living room.

SKILLSPOTLIGHT

Sure, a two-year-old *can walk pretty well. But that doesn't mean her balance is fully developed. As you crawl and wiggle your way through the house, your child is learning how to find and keep her centre of gravity. And she'll be stretching her imagination by pretending she's riding a pretty pony —or perhaps a dashing steed.*

✔	**Balance**
✔	**Gross Motor Skills**
✔	**Imagination**

111

HEAD TO TOES

SINGING THE BODY PARTS

Touch the body part with both hands as you sing its name.

Head, shoulders, knees, and toes.

Knees and toes!

Head, shoulders, knees, and toes.

Knees and toes!

Eyes and ears and mouth and nose, head, shoulders, knees, and toes.

Knees and toes!

Body Awareness	✔
Gross Motor Skills	✔
Listening Skills	✔
Rhythm Exploration	✔
Visual Memory	✔

YOU MAY REMEMBER this song from your own childhood, when you sang it at nursery school or with your friends or parents. It's also a great tune for helping toddlers learn—and remember—the names of body parts.

• Sing "Head, Shoulders, Knees, and Toes" to your child and place both hands on your body parts as you call out the name of each part.

• Keep singing the song over and over, increasing the tempo each time. You'll probably both get mixed up and a bit breathless toward the end—but that's part of the fun!

• Is your toddler having trouble keeping up? Try touching her body as you sing to help her learn how the words and motions fit together.

IF YOUR CHILD ENJOYS THIS ACTIVITY, also try Circle Songs, page 114. ▶

112

24 MONTHS
2
AND UP

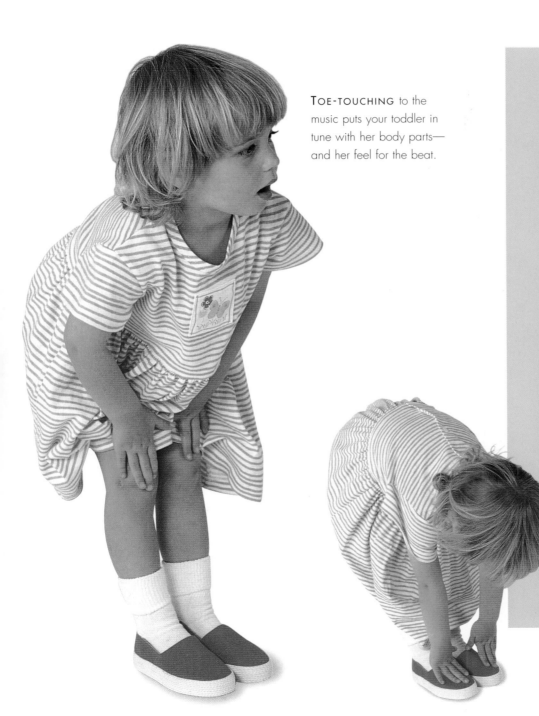

TOE-TOUCHING to the music puts your toddler in tune with her body parts—and her feel for the beat.

RESEARCH REPORT

Not only does music soothe *the savage breast, it seems to perk up the mind as well. Physicist Gordon Shaw and psychologist Frances Rauscher made worldwide headlines in 1993 with a research project showing that college students who listened to Mozart's Sonata for Two Pianos in D Major for ten minutes before a test of their spatial-temporal reasoning ability averaged an eight- or nine-point jump in scores. This finding, along with other studies, so impressed legislators in the U.S. state of Florida that they enacted the "Beethoven's babies law" in 1998, which requires state-funded day care centres to play classical music for thirty minutes every day. While "Head, Shoulders, Knees, and Toes" is a far cry from Mozart, Rauscher believes any complex music (be it classical, jazz, or rock) might enhance brain development.*

CIRCLE SONGS

THESE PERENNIAL FAVOURITES are a perfect choice when your toddler has the urge to move all around. Best of all, there's a camaraderie and joy that comes with circling, singing, and holding hands—whether with Mummy and Daddy or a few cherished friends.

RING-A-RING OF ROSES

Ring-a-ring of roses,
hold hands and walk in a circle
a pocket full of posies,
a-tishoo, a-tishoo
we all fall down!
fall to the ground

The cows are in the pasture,
remain seated in the circle
eating buttercups,
pretend to eat
thunder, lightning,
pound hands on the floor
we all stand up!
stand up quickly

114

THE MULBERRY BUSH

Here we go round the mulberry bush,
hold hands and walk in a circle
the mulberry bush,
the mulberry bush.
Here we go round the mulberry bush,
so early in the morning.

This is the way we clap our hands,
clap hands while standing in a circle
clap our hands,
clap our hands.
This is the way we clap our hands,
so early in the morning.

This is the way we stamp our feet . . .
This is the way we turn around . . .
This is the way we twist and shout . . .
This is the way we reach and stretch . . .
This is the way we run and run . . .
This is the way we sit right down . . .
This is the way we wash our face . . .

LOOBY LOO

Here we go looby loo,
hold hands and walk in a circle
here we go looby light,
here we go looby loo,
all on a Saturday night.
jump up with arms extended skyward

POP GOES THE WEASEL

All around the cobbler's bench,
holding hands, run in a circle
the monkey chased the weasel,
the monkey thought
it was all in fun,
POP goes the weasel!
jump up, then fall
to the ground

U P , DOWN, ALL AROUND:
Circle songs give your toddler a
dizzying array of tunes to move to
and supportive hands to hold.

115

PLAY AQUARIUM

FUN WITH FAKE FISH

SKILLSPOTLIGHT

Playing with a pretend *aquarium gives your child a chance to learn about fish and their strange habits: they swim to get around, after all, and they don't breathe air. The aquarium also gives her an opportunity to exercise her imagination as she plays out a pretend sequence with her plastic fish. And it provides a rich environment for expanding her vocabulary to include words for colours, shapes, textures, and movements.*

Creative Expression	✔
Imagination	✔
Language Development	✔
Sensory Exploration	✔

MOST ADULTS ARE CAPTIVATED by watching fish swimming in a tank. Toddlers like to watch, too, but they seem equally compelled to reach right in and grab a fistful of water, fish, or plant life. You can indulge that desire (and keep the fish safe!) by taking your child to an aquarium that offers touch pools for kids. Or you can create a customized pretend aquarium that your child can play with in her own living room.

• To make a "tank" for your toddler, place a thin layer of blue paper in the bottom of a plastic storage box or dish tub and add large shells, big plastic fish, and fake aquarium plants. Encourage your child to explore the aquatic habitat; talk about textures and colours and how fish swim, glide, and hide. Consider replacing the blue paper with bona fide water if she (and you) are ready for some wet, splashy fun. Also provide her with scoops and strainers for "cleaning" the aquarium.

• Consider setting up a real aquarium—with your child's help—if she's really interested in fish (and be sure to explain that *real* fish can't be held or taken out of the tank). Or take her on field trips to local pet shops to view their aquariums; she'll see not only various types of fish but turtles, frogs, and even sea horses.

A **PRETEND FISH TANK** provides the perfect entrée to the wonderful wet world of a real aquarium. And this fish doesn't mind being high and dry!

IF YOUR CHILD ENJOYS THIS ACTIVITY,
also try Care for the Animals, page 128.

117

24 MONTHS
2
AND UP

SCARF TRICKS

CATCHING THE FLUTTERING FABRIC

SKILLSPOTLIGHT

A two-year-old *is biologically driven to practise gross motor movements of all kinds, such as running, kicking, jumping, and rolling. This activity gives her a new object with which to practise throwing and catching: a silky, fluttering scarf that is as engaging to watch as it is to touch.*

Eye-Foot Coordination	✔
Eye-Hand Coordination	✔
Gross Motor Skills	✔

SHE MAY HAVE almost mastered catching a rolling ball, a wobbling plastic lid, or the family cat. Here's something altogether different to challenge her eye-hand coordination. Gather some brightly coloured, lightweight scarves. Scrunch up a few of them simultaneously in your hand and throw them high in the air, then ask your child to try to catch them as they float and flutter toward the ground. After a few rounds, let her throw some of the scarves while you take a turn at nabbing them mid-air. As she gets older, encourage her to spin around or clap her hands before catching the scarves.

PLUCKING A RAINBOW of colour from the air is as visually stimulating as it is physically challenging—and fun!

24 MONTHS
2
AND UP

RING-A-LING

FUN WITH PHONES

TODDLERS ARE DRAWN to telephones like bears are drawn to honey. But rather than shooing your two-year-old from your carefully programmed cordless telephone, give her a phone of her own. You can use a cast-off from your attic, or buy a fancy toy phone (some even have push buttons that beep!).

Encourage her to use it by holding the receiver to her ear and asking simple questions, such as "What's your name?" "What are you doing today?" and "May I talk to your daddy, please?"

"THIS IS CHRISTINA. Can you visit today?" A pretend phone call with Grandad or Auntie Deb helps your budding socialite learn the give-and-take of conversation.

SKILL SPOTLIGHT

Learning to hold *a conversation, even if it's an imaginary one, helps children exercise their emerging language and social skills. This activity is also a useful way to introduce basic phone etiquette ("Who's calling, please?" or "I'm fine, thank you.") before your toddler starts picking up your phone and talking to your callers.*

✔	**Creative Expression**
✔	**Language Development**
✔	**Self-Concept**
✔	**Social Skills**

IF YOUR CHILD ENJOYS THIS ACTIVITY, also try Doll Talk, page 142.

119

GOOD THROW! It may not be fun for the hippo beanbag, but your little champ will be bowled over by this game of knock 'em down.

BEANBAG BOWLING

24 MONTHS 2 AND UP

LEARNING HOW TO THROW

WHETHER IT'S PUSHING his fork off his high-chair tray or pulling your CDs off the shelves, your toddler delights in putting objects in motion—just to see what will happen (and often to see how you'll react). This is a natural way for toddlers to learn about cause and effect. It's also a good way for them to learn about concepts like gravity and force (not that they need to learn those words—at least not yet). If you're concerned with concepts such as "object fragility," however, channel your child's curiosity about crashes into a game the two of you can play.

• Stack several tall, lightweight plastic bottles, cups, or empty cans. Show your child how to throw a beanbag animal to knock them down. (It will be easier for him to do this from a seated position.) Then take turns tossing the beanbags—but don't bother keeping score.

   • Vary the activity by using different-size balls or even pincushions—without pins, of course—instead of beanbags. Also try seating your child at varying distances from the stack. He'll soon discover that he needs to throw with more force when he's farther away from his target.

   • Once your baby bowler improves his game, ask him to toss the beanbags while standing. And to make the activity more fun for you, encourage him to collect the "pins" he has now learned to blast into all corners of the room!

SKILLSPOTLIGHT

Throwing beanbag toys *or balls at targets helps toddlers develop their eye-hand coordination and adds to their understanding of cause and effect. This activity also helps your child learn to take turns, a skill he'll work on throughout his early years. Taking turns will be crucial to later social interactions, when children need to share to get along with others.*

✔	**Balance**
✔	**Cause & Effect**
✔	**Eye-Hand Coordination**
✔	**Gross Motor Skills**

121

WATERWORKS

AN ACTIVITY FOR THE TUB

SKILLSPOTLIGHT

Water play of any kind can be a wonderful way for parents to engage their toddler's senses. This particular activity provides tactile, visual, and auditory stimulation, as the toddler feels, sees, and hears a stream of water turn into "rain." It also introduces the concepts of empty and full—and helps children learn that water can take many forms and shapes.

Concept Development	✔
Language Development	✔
Sensory Exploration	✔
Tactile Stimulation	✔

SHE LOVES a good rainstorm, and she loves playing in the bath. Now she can create rain in her own tub while learning something about the properties of nature.

• Create "rainmaking" toys by piercing the lids (or bottoms) of yoghurt containers, or use a strainer, a watering can, or a plastic salt shaker.

• Show your toddler how to submerge the containers to fill them with water and then how to empty them. Pouring the water into a colander makes an even bigger shower. Also try gently sprinkling "raindrops" all over her head and body while singing, "Rain, rain go away, come again another day…." Some toddlers will giggle with glee; others may need to wait a few months before they enjoy getting "rained" on.

• Try misting your child with water in a spray bottle (she'll likely try to mist you, too). Or show her how to use a turkey baster and let her squeeze the water into her rainmaking tools.

• An older toddler might like experimenting with a little water dripping from the showerhead—with careful monitoring of the temperature, of course. To make this activity even more enjoyable, climb into the tub with your child and let it pour!

IF YOUR CHILD ENJOYS THIS ACTIVITY, also try Bath Time for Baby, page 126.

THE FUN REALLY FLOWS
when you give your tot the
tools to make a little rain.

WHO ARE WE?

PLAYING DRESS-UP

SKILL SPOTLIGHT

Most two-year-olds *have strong preferences when it comes to their clothing. And many are determined to dress themselves no matter how long it takes. This activity gives them the license to choose their clothes—and the luxury of dressing themselves at their leisure. Role-playing activities also act as dress rehearsals for social interactions later in life.*

Creative Expression	✔
Imagination	✔
Role-Playing	✔
Social Skills	✔

A PRINCESS, A COWBOY, a movie star . . . children love the costume dramas that dressing up inspires.

SHE STARTED TOYING with your scarves, hats, and soft sweaters when she first learned to grab; she headed for your wardrobe as soon as she could crawl. Now it's time to let her go wild with her own wardrobe. Keep a variety of dress-up items on hand (car boot sales and charity shops are great—often inexpensive—sources) and let your child don what she may to be whoever she pleases. Participate in the fun by asking her who she is that day, and invite some of her pals to join in on the act.

124

FOOTSTEP FUN

FOLLOWING THE FEET

EVER SINCE your toddler was a baby, he's been fascinated by his own feet, whether it's the taste of his toes or the look of his first walking shoes. Let him get a whole new view of his feet—as well as strong motor skills practice—by teaching him to follow his own footsteps. Trace the outline of the soles of his shoes onto coloured pieces of paper. Cut out the foot shapes and glue them onto cardboard squares. Place the squares on the floor to form a path, then encourage your pathfinder to place his feet inside each of the silhouettes.

BY ASKING YOUR LITTLE ONE to follow a path of colourful footprints, you provide stepping stones to greater coordination.

SKILLSPOTLIGHT

Following a trail *of any sort requires good balance and coordination. Changing the shape of the path or the distance between the squares, or asking your toddler to jump on and off the path, further challenges that balancing act. Calling out "red," "blue," and "green" as he steps on those colours also helps him expand his vocabulary.*

✔ **Balance**

✔ **Coordination**

✔ **Eye-Foot Coordination**

✔ **Gross Motor Skills**

IF YOUR CHILD ENJOYS THIS ACTIVITY, also try Balancing Act, page 106.

125

BATH TIME FOR BABY

LESSONS IN TENDER, LOVING CARE

SKILLSPOTLIGHT

Two-year-olds *are old enough to play "pretend" and to want some measure of control over their world. This activity lets your child be the parent to her "baby" and also allows her to be the little boss—a great way to practise her social skills and exercise her imagination. Learning to hold a soapy doll and wash its tiny body parts also promotes the development of fine motor skills.*

Body Awareness	✔
Fine Motor Skills	✔
Imagination	✔
Role-Playing	✔
Social Skills	✔

YOUR LITTLE ONE may already be playing "Mummy" or "Daddy" with her dolls and stuffed animals by rocking them, feeding them, and putting them to bed (see Doll Talk, page 142). She'll love giving her baby dolls baths, too; it's a chance for her to be the caregiver at bath time, to learn about keeping the body clean, and to shower her little friends with love.

• Set up a doll's bathtub by filling a basin—or a baby bathtub if you still have one—with warm, soapy water. Provide towels, flannels, soap, and bath toys to make it even more realistic.

• Encourage your toddler to test the water's temperature ("Is it too hot for your doll? Is it too cold?") and to be gentle while washing the doll.

• Point out many of the doll's body parts ("That's her nose! And those are her toes!"). This gives your toddler more practice in labelling her own body parts, a favourite activity at this age.

• Pretend the doll is dirty and encourage her to clean behind the doll's ears, between the toes, and in all the other areas that need washing.

• When the doll is clean, let your toddler dry it with a towel. Then remind her to clean one more thing: her dolly's teeth!

IF YOUR CHILD ENJOYS THIS ACTIVITY, also try Point Out the Parts, page 82.

24 MONTHS
AND UP
2

SCRUB-A-DUB-DUB, it's dolly in the tub! Your two-year-old will love being in charge of her baby's sudsy sponge bath.

RESEARCH REPORT

A few short months ago, *your toddler wasn't able to engage in this type of imaginative play. Kurt Fischer, a Harvard cognitive neuroscientist and educator, has tracked the cranial growth, brain-wave activity, and density of neural connections in children to show that the brain is subject to a series of growth spurts at certain predictable interludes. One such spurt occurs between eighteen and twenty-four months, he says, endowing a child with a capacity for symbolic representation. In other words, for the first time, your child can make the mental leap that an inanimate object (such as her doll) is a "baby" in need of a good washing.*

127

CARE FOR THE ANIMALS

LEARNING TO NURTURE OTHER CREATURES

SKILLSPOTLIGHT

This game of "pretend" teaches your child empathy and lets her practise nurturing others. It also helps build her vocabulary of the animal world: birds have wings, tigers have paws, and an elephant has a trunk. And talking to your toddler about the ways animals get sick ("The horsie ate too much sugar and got a tummy ache.") expands her knowledge of them.

Concept Development	✔
Creative Expression	✔
Fine Motor Skills	✔
Imagination	✔
Role-Playing	✔

SHE LOVES HER ANIMALS (real and stuffed) and she's keen on plasters and the notions of "ouch" and "sick." That means she's more than ready to open up a veterinary practice in her own home. It's all pretend, of course, but she'll enjoy learning how to care for her little friends.

• Help your toddler gather her favourite stuffed and plastic animals for this activity. Make sure the animals are more than 4.5 cm (1¾ inches) in diameter so they won't pose a choking hazard.

• Provide small boxes or plastic baskets for her to use as cages or carriers. She can use napkins or small scarves as blankets.

• Talk to her about the ways in which animals get hurt: how they cut their paws, get pests in their ears, break their wings, or get stomach-aches.

• Help her care for her sick animals by washing and bandaging their wounds, wrapping their broken limbs with gauze, and giving them a clean, quiet place to sleep (plus lots of pats and kind words). A toy doctor's kit will provide helpful instruments for conducting a thorough exam—and treatment—of her ailing friends, too.

IF YOUR CHILD ENJOYS THIS ACTIVITY, also try Animal Actors, page 180.

"Is the pony hurt?"

HELPING HER PLAY
pretend vet is a natural
way to nurture her knowl-
edge of all living things.

129

THE MANY FORMS OF PLAY

WHILE THIS BOOK emphasizes the playful inter-actions between a parent and child, it's also important to understand how a toddler will play with peers. One-year-olds are primarily involved in solitary play, busy as they are explor-ing a world that is totally new to them. They are curious about other children, however, and often will imitate their actions or the noises they make. As they get a little older, toddlers begin engaging in parallel play—that is, two or more youngsters playing with similar toys or activities side by side but without much interaction, such as building block towers individually. Around age two, as child psychologist Penelope Leach notes in *Your Baby and Child,* "Toddlers increasingly need the companionship of other children." Most adore tak-ing part in play groups, but their ability to share toys or to indulge in mannerly back-and-forth exchanges is still a little precarious. As they approach their third birthday, true cooperative play begins to emerge—two toddlers will build a single block tower together, for example—although there are still likely to be standoffs over treasured playthings or the attention of beloved adults.

These early play encounters plant the seeds for acquiring important attributes such as empathy, self-control, sharing, fairness, and self-esteem, and they help cultivate much-needed tools for dealing with different social situations. As Dr. Benjamin Spock explained in *Baby and Child Care,* "In play, children . . . learn how to get along with other chil-dren and adults of different personalities, how to enjoy give-and-take, how to solve conflicts." These are valuable lessons indeed, and ones that parents can foster by providing plenty of opportunities for play with other children. ■

MAGIC CUPS

24 MONTHS
2
AND UP

A CHALLENGING MEMORY GAME

THIS TODDLER ACTIVITY is a step up from peekaboo, but operates on the same principle. First it's here, then it's gone, then it's back again—but only if your toddler remembers where it was! To start the game, hide a small toy under one of three cups while your child is watching. Then move the cups around and ask her to guess which one conceals the toy.

- If you've seen street entertainers play this game, you know it can be confusing, even for adults. So don't move the cups too quickly or else she won't be able to keep track of her toy.

SKILLSPOTLIGHT

When your toddler *was a baby, you could cover up a toy and she would forget it ever existed. Now she understands that the covered object is still there—this is called object permanence—and she's delighted to find it. By asking her to concentrate on one cup as it moves, you encourage her to re-call the toy and you help sharpen her visual memory.*

✔ **Problem Solving**

✔ **Visual Memory**

WHICH CUP HIDES THE YELLOW ducky? She'll love trying to keep tabs—especially if you applaud her when she's right.

131

BEEP, BEEP

PLAYING WITH LORRIES AND CARS

SKILLSPOTLIGHT

Playing with toy cars *is a great way for your toddler to exercise her imagination, and it gives her a chance to imitate a mundane part of your adult world: driving the car. (Don't worry; it's interesting to her!) It also lets her develop the fine motor skills of pushing and pulling and teaches her to discern noises in her everyday world.*

Creative Expression	✔
Fine Motor Skills	✔
Imagination	✔
Language Development	✔

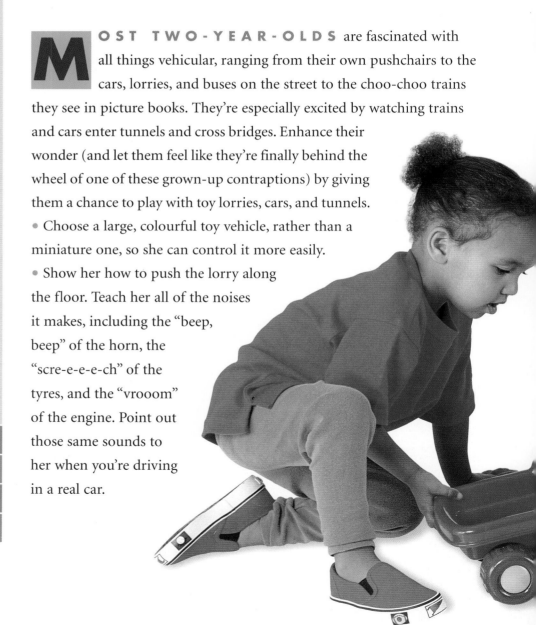

MOST TWO-YEAR-OLDS are fascinated with all things vehicular, ranging from their own pushchairs to the cars, lorries, and buses on the street to the choo-choo trains they see in picture books. They're especially excited by watching trains and cars enter tunnels and cross bridges. Enhance their wonder (and let them feel like they're finally behind the wheel of one of these grown-up contraptions) by giving them a chance to play with toy lorries, cars, and tunnels.

• Choose a large, colourful toy vehicle, rather than a miniature one, so she can control it more easily.

• Show her how to push the lorry along the floor. Teach her all of the noises it makes, including the "beep, beep" of the horn, the "scre-e-e-ch" of the tyres, and the "vrooom" of the engine. Point out those same sounds to her when you're driving in a real car.

132

• Cut holes in both ends of a big cardboard box to make a tunnel and show her how to push the lorry through it. Talk about the different parts of the lorry (steering wheel, tyres) and explain why she might need to "turn on" the headlights when she drives into the dark tunnel. Also see if she can guess which part of the lorry will come out of the tunnel first—the front or the back.

STEER HER ENERGY into a little creative car play, and watch those motor skills grow.

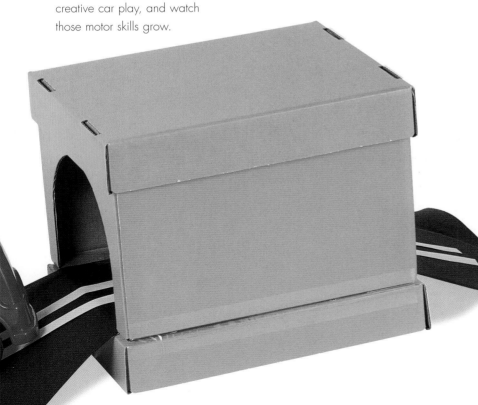

RESEARCH REPORT

A toddler's *apparently boundless enthusiasm for play reflects the fact that she is in a unique and wondrous period of development. A child's brain at age two years consumes twice as much metabolic energy as an adult's, and it possesses twice as many synapses (the connections between nerve cells that convey the electrical impulses needed for all the body's functions, including cognition). "Children are biologically primed for learning during this time,"* state neurologist Ann Barnet and her co-author and husband, Richard, in their book The Youngest Minds. *This golden window of opportunity lasts only until age ten or so, when the brain starts to lose the synaptic connections that haven't yet been put to use.*

DRIVE THE FIRE ENGINE

A FAVOURITE MOVEMENT SONG

to the *tune* of **"Ten Little Indians"**

Hurry, hurry,
drive the fire engine,
make driving motions
hurry, hurry,
drive the fire engine,
hurry, hurry,
drive the fire engine,
ding, ding, ding, ding, ding!
swing hand as if ringing a bell

Hurry, hurry,
climb the ladder,
pretend to climb a ladder
hurry, hurry,
climb the ladder,
hurry, hurry,
climb the ladder,
ding, ding, ding, ding, ding!

Hurry, hurry,
squirt the water,
make squirting motions
hurry, hurry,
squirt the water,
hurry, hurry,
squirt the water,
ding, ding, ding, ding, ding!

Language Development	✔
Role-Playing	✔

RING THE BELL! Sound the alarm! This fast-paced song lets your lorry-loving tyke pretend to drive the biggest, brightest vehicle around—a fire engine—while letting him play one of the most exciting roles in town. Face your child while you teach him the hand gestures, or have him stand with his back to you and help him do them himself. If he is ready to act out the role of a fireman, find a heavy-duty cardboard box, paint it bright red, and push him around in it as you sing "Hurry, Hurry, Drive the Fire Engine" and he makes the motions.

YOUR LITTLE FIREMAN will think this is the hottest game of all when he realizes he gets to drive the fire engine and put out the imaginary fire with his pretend hose.

PURSE TREASURES

24 MONTHS 2 AND UP

EXPLORING GOODIES IN THE BAG

GRANTED, A TODDLER'S boundless curiosity about the treasures in your purse or briefcase is adorable. But it can lead to chaos (like lost credit cards) and even danger (opened pillboxes and pointy pencils). Safely encourage her explorations by giving her a purse of her very own. Fill it with harmless objects such as those she might find in your bag: a comb, keys, mirror, notepad—even a wallet. Encourage her to find things without looking ("Can you feel the keys in there?"), or ask her to name each item as she pulls it out.

SKILLSPOTLIGHT

You can enrich *your child's understanding of all the items in her purse by explaining the use of each object as she pulls it out ("I'm glad you found the car keys. Now we can drive to the supermarket." Or, "Would you like to comb your hair with that?"). Frequently changing the objects in the purse further challenges your child's identifying skills.*

✔	**Concept Development**
✔	**Language Development**
✔	**Listening Skills**
✔	**Tactile Discrimination**

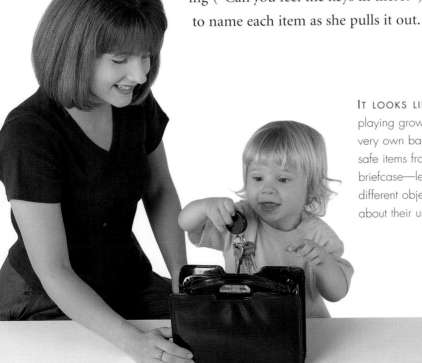

IT LOOKS LIKE she's just playing grown-up. But her very own bag—filled with safe items from a parent's briefcase—lets her explore different objects and learn about their uses.

TOUCH AND TELL

WHAT'S IN THE PILLOWCASE?

SKILL SPOTLIGHT

Learning to describe *the objects in his world helps your child feel some measure of control over them. It also helps him develop his language skills. And adding a tactile component to his developing visual memory helps him understand objects in a three-dimensional way.*

Concept Development	✔
Language Development	✔
Listening Skills	✔
Problem Solving	✔
Tactile Discrimination	✔

YOUR TODDLER is getting into just about everything now, mostly because he's compelled to explore how everything feels, tastes, sounds, looks, and moves. Help him investigate and identify the sensations of different shapes and textures with this variation of the classic show-and-tell game.

• Place a familiar object such as his toy lorry, ball, doll, or favourite spoon or cup inside a pillowcase or canvas bag.

• Ask your child to reach into the pillowcase (no peeking!) and feel the object. Then ask him to guess what it is. (He may need to guess more than once.) If he can't, tell him what it is before he grows too frustrated.

• Pull out the object and talk to him about its tactile characteristics. Introduce the concepts of hard and soft, fuzzy and smooth.

• Put another toy inside and repeat the exercise. Encourage him to use the words you've introduced as he's trying to guess what the toy is.

• To vary the game, let him hide a toy in the pillowcase so you can play detective. Also try putting an object inside and asking your young sleuth to guess what it is by feeling it from *outside* the pillowcase.

IF YOUR CHILD ENJOYS THIS ACTIVITY, also try Mystery Sounds, page 141.

"Look! It's my cup!"

HE'LL GET A FEEL for textures and learn to name those sensations in this hands-on guessing game.

137

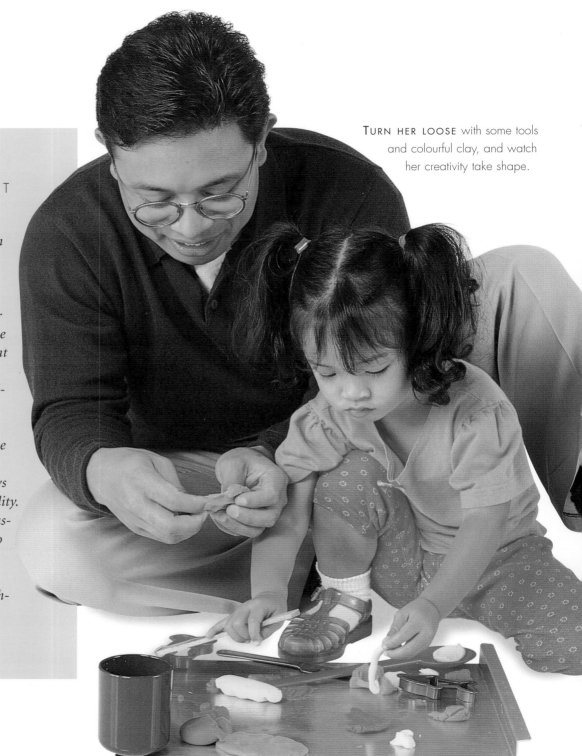

TURN HER LOOSE with some tools and colourful clay, and watch her creativity take shape.

RESEARCH REPORT

Squishing and shaping
modelling clay does more than encourage the budding artist in your child. By allowing her to handle these and other tactile delights, you're helping her develop "knowledge of how the world works and proficiency at using different materials," states Esther Thelen, a psychologist at Indiana University. Educational psychologist Jane Healy is another believer in the benefits of clay, sand, finger paint, and mud, which she says help refine a child's tactile ability. She also offers this advice to fastidious parents: "If you tend to be fanatic about cleanliness, close your eyes and imagine little [neural] dendrites branching inside that muddy head."

PLAY WITH CLAY

24 MONTHS
2
AND UP

MAKING SHAPES AND SCULPTURES

YOU PROBABLY HAVE fond memories of moulding clay into silly shapes, and now your two-year-old is ready to dive into the colourful stuff. Purchase non-toxic modelling clay in any toy shop or make a few colourful batches yourself (see the recipe for clay at right). Provide ample working space and a few safe tools, such as a rolling pin, a potato masher, and biscuit cutters. Then let the sculpting begin.

• Most young children prefer to experiment with mushing the clay into abstract shapes. Guide her in manipulating the clay by rolling it into a ball and letting her smash it. Or make a long roll that she can tear into pieces and press back together.

• Show your child how simple shapes such as circles, squares, and triangles fit together to make recognizable objects like faces, hats, or trees.

• To store the clay, gather several airtight containers and mark each lid with the same colour as the clay it contains. When she's done playing with the clay, ask her to put it in its appropriate container.

MAKING YOUR OWN

Mix 1 cup flour, 1 cup salt, 1 tablespoon cream of tartar, 1 cup water, and 1 tablespoon vegetable oil. Simmer in a pan until clay begins to pull away from the pan's sides. When cool, add 5 drops of food colouring, and knead until smooth.

SKILLSPOTLIGHT

Playing with modelling clay *allows your child to experience shapes and textures in three dimensions. In addition, manipulating the clay stimulates the senses and builds fine motor skills. Help increase your child's vocabulary by teaching her the words for basic colours, shapes, and textures.*

✔	**Cause & Effect**
✔	**Creative Expression**
✔	**Fine Motor Skills**
✔	**Language Development**
✔	**Sensory Exploration**

◀ *IF YOUR CHILD ENJOYS THIS ACTIVITY,*
also try Sand Skills, page 68.

IF THE SHOE FITS

SORTING SHOES OF SEVERAL SIZES

SKILLSPOTLIGHT

This easy-to-assemble project *allows toddlers to practise their early sorting skills and make discoveries about size and materials. As you talk together, your toddler's use of language expands; when you ask him to guess or make assumptions about the different shoes and their uses, you encourage the development of his problem-solving abilities.*

Classifying Skills	✔
Language Development	✔

IF YOUR CHILD ENJOYS THIS ACTIVITY, also try Car Capers, page 166.

MANY CLASSIFYING ACTIVITIES are too frustrating for younger toddlers, but by age two to two-and-a-half, most children are eager to perform a fairly simple sorting task—especially if it involves playing with Mummy's or Daddy's shoes. Put two or three pairs of shoes on a table, separating each shoe from its mate. Choose shoes of distinct sizes and types, such as adult boots, baby shoes, and your fuzzy slippers. Ask your child which shoes match. As he searches for the mate, talk about the types of shoes, whom they fit, and what they're used for. Some toddlers find it easier to sort if they have shoe boxes to put the pairs into.

WHICH SHOES BELONG together? Toddlers can try to successfully combine pairs of family footwear in a challenging game of mix-and-match.

140

MYSTERY SOUNDS

24 MONTHS
2
AND UP

FINDING THE HIDDEN NOISE

WHAT'S THAT SOUND? Where is it coming from? Those are the questions to pose to young detectives in this game of auditory hide-and-seek. Use a long-playing musical toy or other noisemaking item (such as a kitchen timer, clock, or metronome) and hide it on a low shelf or table—or behind a cupboard door. Search together with your child to locate the source of the sound and retrieve the object. As you hunt, ask your toddler to try to guess what toy or object is making the mysterious sound.

USING HER EARS to find the source of a sound may become a young sleuth's favourite guessing game.

SKILLSPOTLIGHT

Young children love *guessing games, and this one helps fine-tune auditory skills. Locating an object by listening to a sound teaches your toddler to find an answer through the process of elimination—and it reinforces the notion that a thoughtful guess is part of the learning process.*

✓ **Listening Skills**

✓ **Problem Solving**

IF YOUR CHILD ENJOYS THIS ACTIVITY, also try Mighty Megaphones, page 169. ▶

DOLL TALK

LEARNING TO NURTURE

Toddlers learn *to be kind to others—whether they are animals or people—often by watching their parents' behaviour. Participating in your child's doll (or animal) play gives you the opportunity to model appropriate words and gestures. It also gives her a chance to feel confident about her emerging feelings of gentleness and love.*

Creative Expression	✔
Fine Motor Skills	✔
Imagination	✔
Listening Skills	✔
Social Skills	✔

SEEING A TODDLER'S TENDERNESS toward the dolls, teddies, and other cuddlies in her world is truly touching. Her enthusiasm, however, may sometimes make her a bit too rough—especially with animals or other children. You can help refine her nurturing abilities by interacting with your child as she plays with her pretend friends.

• Give your child a favourite doll or stuffed animal to hold. Suggest that she gently brush the doll's hair or rock it in her arms. Or help her learn to pat animals by showing her how on a plush toy.

• Tell her that the doll or teddy bear is cold, and ask her to comfort it by putting shoes and socks and warm clothes on the doll (she may need help with poppers and buttons) or a blanket over the plush toy.

• Then suggest that she feed her doll or pet because it hasn't eaten all day and must be quite hungry. She can offer it pretend food, or give her a spoon and a small dish of cereal or raisins, which are easy to clean up.

• Join your child in singing a favourite lullaby to her charge while helping her rock it to sleep, then ask her to gently tuck it into bed.

*IF YOUR CHILD ENJOYS THIS ACTIVITY,
also try Bath Time for Baby, page 126.*

RESEARCH REPORT

While many adults *still struggle with the finer points of grammar, we might be humbled to learn that 90 per cent of the sentences spoken by the average three-year-old are grammatically correct. The mistakes they make usually result from an overly zealous application of the rules. For example, in English we usually indicate plurals by adding an "s" or "es" to the end of a noun—rivers, churches—and we use the suffix "ed" to convey the past tense of verbs—patted, changed, kissed. So why do we laugh at a toddler who says, "I want three mouses" or "You gived me a doll"? Hey, she's just following the rules!*

WHEN DADDY SHOWS his daughter how to care for her doll, he provides an important lesson in nurturing others.

COLOUR CLUSTERS

A SORTING, SPINNING, AND COUNTING ACTIVITY

SKILLSPOTLIGHT

This elementary abacus *enhances your toddler's ability to categorize objects by helping him identify different colours and sizes. It also provides a great opportunity to introduce your child to comparison words, such as big, bigger, and biggest.*

Classifying Skills	✔
Concept Development	✔
Coordination	✔
Language Development	✔

COLOURFUL, REVOLVING BALLS on a rope are sure to catch toddlers' eyes, as they love both bright colours and spinning motions. But besides being fun, this activity can teach your little one some pretty big concepts. To start, thread a thin rope through a group of coloured balls with holes (available at many toy stores) and tie the rope firmly between two chairs. Show your toddler how to spin the balls and slide them from one end of the rope to the other. Then ask him to spin only a particular colour or only the large balls.

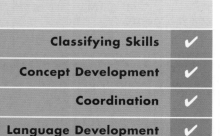

MAKING THE BRIGHT BALLS spin quickly is fun, but so is learning to identify blue and red, large and small, and more and less.

WATER TARGETS

30 MONTHS
2½
AND UP

MAKING A SPLASH LANDING

WATER, BALLS, THROWING, splashing... the elements in this activity may get you and your toddler a bit wet, but she'll enjoy it so much you won't mind. Find two or three big plastic bowls or pots and fill them halfway with water. Gather an assortment of small balls, preferably ones that float (plastic or tennis balls work well). Ask your child to throw the balls into the water targets. Count how many balls she can land inside each bowl and be sure to applaud every attempt, even when she misses. As she gets better at this activity, increase the challenge by having her stand farther away from the water-filled bowls.

YOUR LITTLE PITCHER makes a big splash when she gets the ball in—and she fine-tunes her coordination skills as she aims for her water targets.

SKILLSPOTLIGHT

This water game *helps build your toddler's eye-hand coordination and gross motor skills. The activity is also a fun way to introduce your toddler to counting ("That's one in, two in. Look! Three balls in the water!").*

✔ **Coordination**

✔ **Counting Concepts**

✔ **Eye-Hand Coordination**

✔ **Gross Motor Skills**

IF YOUR CHILD ENJOYS THIS ACTIVITY, *also try Up It Goes!, page 152.* ▶

145

PAINT PRIMER

INSPIRING THE ARTIST WITHIN

At thirty months, *he's only just beginning to realize that he can create something, whether it's a scribble with a crayon or a painting covered with brush strokes. Letting him paint what he wants helps him feel confident about expressing himself visually. Turning everyday objects into artistic tools develops his creativity as well as his fine motor control and eye-hand coordination.*

Creative Expression	✔
Eye-Hand Coordination	✔
Fine Motor Skills	✔
Tactile Stimulation	✔

HE'S NOT OLD ENOUGH to paint still lifes or landscapes, and you may not recognize much of what he creates, but every toddler has an inner artist that's just itching to get out. Help set that creative spirit free by providing paints and simple tools that even the smallest hands can handle.

• Set out several colours of non-toxic (such as tempera) paints in small bowls or tins. Collect a variety of painting tools, too, including paintbrushes, dish scrubbers, and sponges cut into shapes.

• Show your child how to dip his utensils into the paint and to roll or brush them on the paper. Then let him experiment with colours and designs. Remember, there's no right or wrong way at this age—so let him make whatever inspires him, not what you want him to make.

• If your child seems to want some guidance from you, paint a few large shapes (circles, squares, triangles, rectangles) and let him colour them—but do not expect him to stay inside the lines.

• Don't forgo the fun because you're afraid of mess and fuss: tape large sheets of paper onto an easily washable surface (such as the kitchen floor or table) and pop your junior Picasso in the bath when he's done.

IF YOUR CHILD ENJOYS THIS ACTIVITY, also try Colourful Collages, page 160.

30 MONTHS
2½
AND UP

"LOOK WHAT I MADE, DADDY!
It's a fire engine!" Broadening your
child's creative palette is as easy
as putting paint to paper.

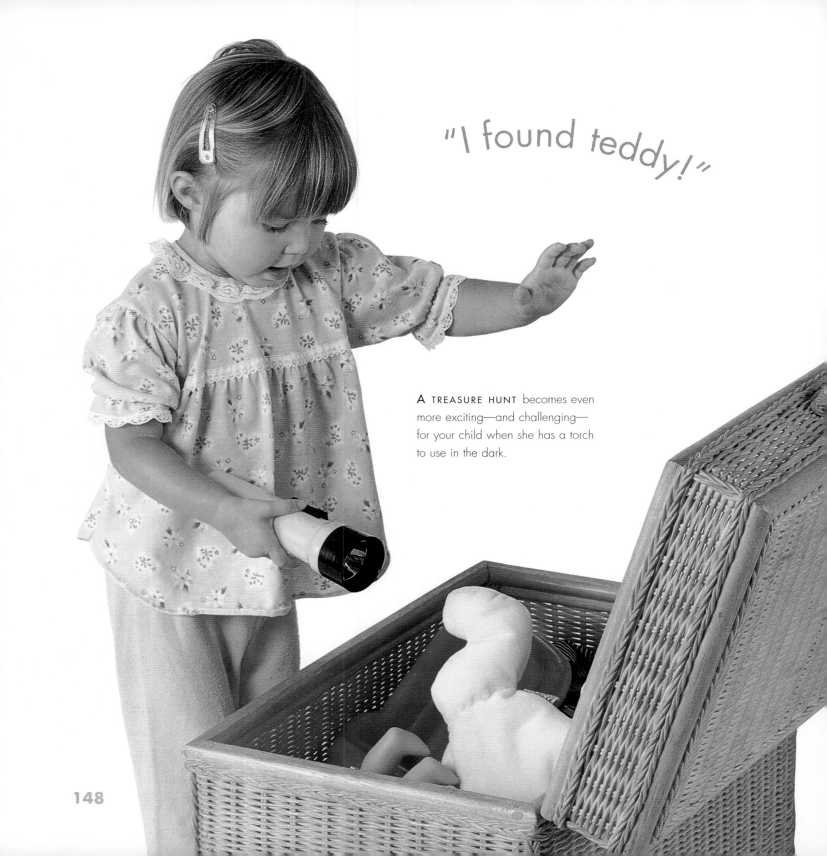

"I found teddy!"

A **TREASURE HUNT** becomes even more exciting—and challenging— for your child when she has a torch to use in the dark.

148

FLASHLIGHT FUN

FINDING HIDDEN TOYS IN THE DARK

WIELDING A TORCH sparks wonder in most toddlers: the tool gives them control over the dark and changes the look of everything around them.

• Start this activity in the evening by hiding one of your child's favourite items, such as a doll, a book, or her beloved teddy bear. Limit the hunting area to one or two rooms so it won't be too difficult for her to find the hidden treasure.

• Tell your toddler what to look for, turn off (or just dim) the lights, and hand her a lightweight torch. (You may have to show her how to use it at first.) Equip yourself with a torch, too.

• Keep the game lively and silly by providing her with several clues if need be: "You're getting warmer, warmer, warmer! Oops! Now you're cooling down." If she starts to get a little frustrated, use the beam of your own torch to help guide her to the hiding place.

• This is an ideal activity for a toddler to play with an older sibling or a group of kids, because you can hide several objects at one time—some in harder places than others—and it's a great spectacle to watch the children waving their bright beams of light at one another.

◀ *IF YOUR CHILD ENJOYS THIS ACTIVITY, also try Purse Treasures, page 135.*

SKILL SPOTLIGHT

Searching for an object *presents a problem that your child has to concentrate on in order to solve. The first step, of course, is to listen to your description of the hidden object, which involves comprehension skills. Then she has to think about places that aren't immediately visible to her—a type of abstract thinking that is a big step for a young child. This night-time game may also allay fears and negative feelings that children often have about darkness.*

✓	**Listening Skills**
✓	**Problem Solving**
✓	**Social Skills**
✓	**Visual Memory**

NATURE VS. NURTURE

DO WE COME into this world imprinted with immutable abilities, foibles, and personality traits? Or are we born blank slates, waiting for the environment to etch its effect on our psyches? For many scientists, the new influx of brain research has settled the age-old question of nature versus nurture once and for all. The verdict? It's a draw.

For decades, behavioural studies have suggested that some traits, such as aggressiveness, shyness, and a willingness to take risks, have a genetic origin. But just when Mother Nature seemed to be the winner in the ancient debate, neurologists demonstrated how unfinished the human brain is at birth and how environmental factors exert powerful influences on a person's disposition—even altering the shape of the brain in some cases. Scientists in the 1990s have reconciled these two competing forces by concluding that while people are indeed born with certain tendencies and abilities, the degree to which those traits are manifested depends a great deal on what they're exposed to, especially during early childhood. As neurologist Ann Barnet states in her book *The Youngest Minds,* "Current estimates made by behavioural geneticists for the relative influence of heritable factors and environment are about 50-50."

This split has important implications for parents. For one thing, it means that if a child is innately inclined to some particular behaviour, parents can work with her to overcome that tendency—helping her become more outgoing if she's shy, for example, or instilling a little impulse control if she's inclined to take too many risks. Conversely, it also suggests that even if a child is born with certain gifts, such as outstanding musical or artistic ability, those talents might never be realized if there's no opportunity for them to flourish. ■

HEY MR. JUMPING JACK

30 MONTHS
2½
AND UP

WIGGLE AND SHAKE TO A BEAT

GET YOUR LITTLE ONE giggling and wiggling to this upbeat chant that encourages rhythm and movement. Hold your child on your lap, facing you, and then tap out a rhythm with your feet as you say the words. When Mr. Jumping Jack jumps high, lift your toddler up high; when he jumps low, give him just a little lift. For the second verse, wiggle your child gently as you lift him high and low (hard shaking is dangerous). Add your own verses and movements—clapping, flapping, and waving, for example. And when your toddler is steady on his feet, let him jump and wiggle on his own as you chant and clap.

SECURE in Mummy's arms, your toddler will laugh out loud as he soars up and down to the words of this cheery chant.

Hey Mr. Jumping Jack,
a funny old man,
he jumps and he jumps
whenever he can.
He jumps way up high,
he jumps way down low,
and he jumps and he jumps
wherever he goes.

Come on and jump!

Hey Mr. Jumping Jack,
a funny old man,
he wiggles and he wiggles whenever he can.
He wiggles way up high,
he wiggles way down low,
and he wiggles and he wiggles
wherever he goes.

Come on and wiggle!

✓ **Listening Skills**

✓ **Rhythm Exploration**

IF YOUR CHILD ENJOYS THIS ACTIVITY,
also try Teddy Bear Tunes, page 156.

151

UP IT GOES!

A BALL-AND-PARACHUTE GAME

SKILL SPOTLIGHT

This game challenges *your toddler's coordination and visual acuity. To toss the ball straight up, she has to try to raise the blanket in sync with you. To catch it squarely on the blanket, she needs to keep her eye on the ball as it comes back down. This activity takes planning and some sense of cooperation with her partner— and she may need to practise it several times before she catches on.*

Cause & Effect	✔
Eye-Foot Coordination	✔
Eye-Hand Coordination	✔

◀ *IF YOUR CHILD ENJOYS THIS ACTIVITY, also try Beach-Ball Catch, page 105.*

SUMMER OR WINTER, indoors or out, a beach ball—or another very lightweight ball—makes for all kinds of merriment when there's a toddler around. To play this game, you and your child hold opposite ends of a blanket or mini-parachute. Place a beach ball in the centre and toss it up in the air, trying to catch it in the parachute as it comes down again. Start with gentle tosses so the ball doesn't go too high. As your toddler's coordination improves, bounce the ball higher and higher.

SHE FOLLOWS the bouncing ball in this delightful game that exercises her ability to coordinate muscle movements with motion.

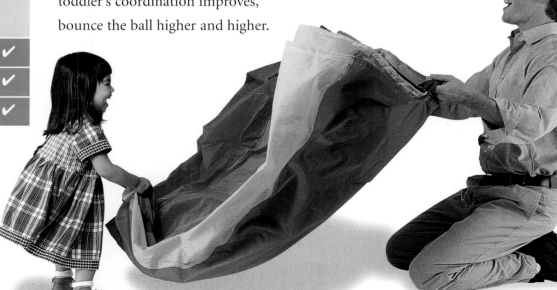

PAPER PUZZLE

FITTING THE BIG PIECES TOGETHER

IF YOUR CHILD is already happily playing with wooden puzzles and shape sorters, it might be a prime time to enhance his ability to understand and organize shapes spatially by creating an elementary puzzle for him. Find an engaging, colourful picture of something your toddler might like—an animal, a lorry, a baby, or a favourite food, for instance. (Magazines are rich sources for large photographs.) Then glue the image onto a letter-size piece of paper or cardboard. Cut the picture into four large sections. Now help him rearrange the pieces to put the picture back together again. When he's figured that out, you can make the puzzle more difficult by cutting it into smaller pieces.

PUTTING TWO AND TWO together to make a butterfly is just the kind of puzzle your toddler is now ready to tackle.

SKILLSPOTLIGHT

This activity allows *your toddler to exercise his understanding of spatial relations. It also lets him create—and re-create—a picture that he likes (a test of his visual memory skills), which will give him the confidence to eventually try more difficult puzzles.*

✔	Concept Development
✔	Problem Solving
✔	Size & Shape Discrimination
✔	Visual Discrimination
✔	Visual Memory

153

COMMON SCENTS

AN ODYSSEY OF ODOURS

SHE SMILES WHEN EATING a biscuit and purses her little lips at the sight of broccoli, so you know she has a discriminating palate. But how's her sense of smell? Help her learn to match aroma to food with this simple sniffing game.

• Gather several strongly scented foods that your child already knows, such as chocolate-chip cookies, oranges, and onions.

• Blindfold her with a handkerchief or scarf (or just cover her eyes with your hand). Then ask her to take a big sniff (no peeking!) and guess what the smells are. After she guesses, let her taste the food to better match different smells with different tastes.

• As she masters this activity, choose foods with more subtle aromas. For example, see if she can distinguish between a peach and an apple, a biscuit and a cake, or a lemon and an orange.

• You can do this with outside smells, too. Test her olfactory memory on flowers, pine needles, damp dirt, and common herbs.

• Or ask your toddler to identify smells she might encounter in the neighbourhood, such as fresh bread in a bakery, barbecued chicken in a restaurant, or summer fruits at a market stall.

IF YOUR CHILD ENJOYS THIS ACTIVITY, also try Touch and Tell, page 136.

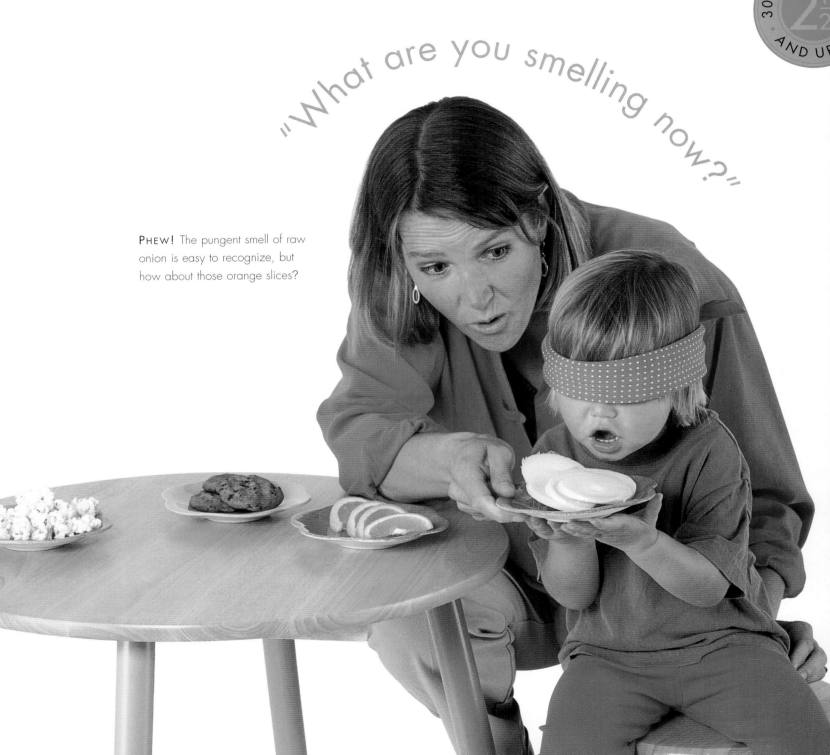

30 MONTHS
AND UP
2 1/2

"What are you smelling now?"

PHEW! The pungent smell of raw onion is easy to recognize, but how about those orange slices?

TEDDY BEAR TUNES

TODDLERS LOVE teddy bears—and the rhythm and repetition of these teddy tunes give them a timeless appeal. With your child on your knee, bounce her gently to the beat of these songs while encouraging her to sing along—or join her (and her plush toys) in acting out the appropriate gestures.

THE BEAR

to the tune of **"For He's a Jolly Good Fellow"**

**The bear went over the mountain,
the bear went over the mountain,
the bear went over the mountain,
to see what she could see.**

**To see what she could see,
To see what she could see.**

**The bear went over the mountain,
the bear went over the mountain,
the bear went over the mountain,
to see what she could see.**

TEDDY BEAR, TEDDY BEAR

Teddy bear, teddy bear, turn around.
*turn around in circles with your child
as you teach her this chant*

**Teddy bear, teddy bear,
touch the ground.**
touch the floor

**Teddy bear, teddy bear,
show your shoe.**
bring one foot forward

**Teddy bear, teddy bear,
crawl right through.**
let your child crawl between your legs

MARCHING BEARS

 to the *tune* of **"The Saints Go Marching In"**

**Oh when the bears
go marching in,
oh when the bears go marching in,
oh, how I want to be a big teddy,
when the bears go marching in.**
march in place with your child

**Oh when the bears
go jumping in,
oh when the bears go jumping in,
oh, how I want to be a big teddy,
when the bears go jumping in.**
jump up and down

**Oh when the bears
go wiggling in . . .**
wiggle your body

**Oh when the bears
go tiptoeing in . . .**
tiptoe around the room

**Oh when the bears
go hopping in . . .**
hop up and down

BEARS ARE SLEEPING

 to the *tune* of **"Frère Jacques"**

**Bears are sleeping,
bears are sleeping,
in their caves, in their caves.
Waiting for the springtime,
waiting for the springtime.
Shh! Shh! Shh!
Shh! Shh! Shh!**

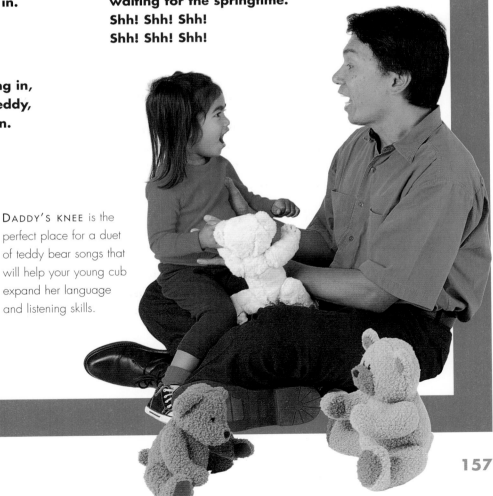

DADDY'S KNEE is the perfect place for a duet of teddy bear songs that will help your young cub expand her language and listening skills.

157

ON TARGET!

LANDING ON THE MARK

SKILLSPOTLIGHT

The act of jumping *works muscles on both sides of the body, thereby increasing bilateral coordination. This provides a good counterpoint to activities, such as rolling a ball, that work only one side of the body. Jumping also improves eye-foot coordination and balance in an older toddler: she needs to put her feet where she's looking and then she has to try to stay upright after landing.*

Balance	✔
Eye-Foot Coordination	✔
Gross Motor Skills	✔
Spatial Awareness	✔

JUMPING IS A BIG accomplishment for toddlers, one that takes coordination, strength, and a dash of courage. It's also a skill that thrills: just observe the joy on your puddle jumper's face after leaping into a big pool of rainwater. You can help improve her form and aim and boost her confidence by setting up jumping target practice using a stable stool, block, or another safe launching pad (just be sure she lands on a soft or cushioned surface).

• Use a large piece of coloured paper or a coloured paper plate as a target, and stick it to the ground with strong packaging tape so it won't slip when she lands. Encourage your child to jump directly onto the target—this will likely take some practice. Applaud her every attempt.

• As your toddler's abilities increase, make the target smaller. Or ask her to jump from a greater (though still safe) height.

• Some children may be nervous about bounding into space this way. Soothe her fears by showing her how to jump—or hold her hand as she makes the leap. Once she becomes confident in her jumping abilities, she'll want to aim for the target again and again.

IF YOUR CHILD ENJOYS THIS ACTIVITY, also try Turn Around, page 163.

READY? SET. GO! This aerial joyride is a jumping-off point for building strong muscles and eye-foot coordination.

RESEARCH REPORT

Enriching experiences *such as assembling a collage provide children with creative stimulation that is vital to their development. Researchers at Baylor College of Medicine in Houston, Texas, found that children deprived of playthings and playmates (and of nurturing caregivers) have brains 20 to 30 per cent smaller than normal. To provide the proper stimulation, parents needn't stock up on all sorts of techno-gadgets and expensive toys; an extensive study conducted at the University of Alabama found that the basics, such as art supplies, blocks, and puzzles, were still the best at promoting cognitive and physical development.*

COLOURFUL COLLAGES

COLLECTING INTRIGUING IMAGES

EVEN AT THIS EARLY AGE, your child has distinct likes and dislikes. He may be fascinated by music, for instance, or animals, or occupations such as gardening and cooking. Encourage him to enjoy his natural interests by helping him create a fun collage made from an assortment of pictures.

• Collect colourful pictures of his current passion from magazines, newspapers, even catalogues, and place them in a big basket or bowl.

• Invite your toddler to look through them and talk about the pictures as he picks them up. Ask him to name the objects he sees (for example, a violin, a whale, a flower, a blueberry muffin).

• Ask him to pick out his favourite pictures. Place them on a large sheet of heavyweight paper, such as coloured paper.

• Using children's (non-toxic) glue, show him how to put glue onto the back of a picture, then press it down onto the paper to make a collage.

• Once you both have completed the collage, hang it somewhere visible, such as in his bedroom, on the refrigerator, or even in the front hallway. Children's art should be seen—not hidden!

SKILLSPOTLIGHT

Letting your child *select his own pictures for a collage gives him a chance to practise expressing his preferences. Encouraging him to discuss the images is a way to help build his vocabulary. And teaching him to handle glue and sticky pieces of paper aids him in developing his fine motor skills.*

✔	**Creative Expression**
✔	**Fine Motor Skills**
✔	**Language Development**
✔	**Visual Discrimination**

"I LIKE DOLPHINS because they live in the ocean." Learn more about your child while creating a work of art that reflects his personality and preferences.

IF YOUR CHILD ENJOYS THIS ACTIVITY, also try Paper Puzzle, page 153.

161

30 MONTHS
2½
AND UP

BEAUTIFUL BOX

DECORATING A TOY CHEST

SKILLSPOTLIGHT.

This project nurtures *a toddler's creative spirit while encouraging her to express herself on something other than flat paper. By combining drawing, painting, colouring, and collage, it introduces her to several different artistic media. This activity also polishes fine motor skills and can help develop communication skills, especially if parents engage their children in a discussion as they're decorating the box together.*

Creative Expression	✔
Fine Motor Skills	✔
Social Skills	✔

TAKE YOUR TODDLER'S natural (albeit elementary) artistic abilities to a new dimension by helping her decorate a box for her toy treasures. Use a plain or coloured cardboard box (or cover a printed box with white paper). Give your child non-permanent markers and crayons for drawing lines and circles on the box; help her glue glitter, ribbons, or paper cutouts on it as well. You can start with a theme (such as the sea) and encourage her to elaborate on that topic with stickers of waves, fish, boats, and beach balls. When she's done, write her name on her special box.

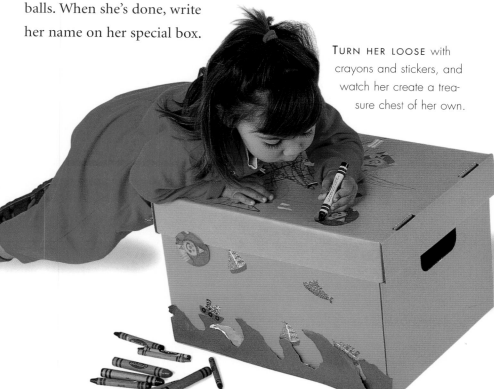

TURN HER LOOSE with crayons and stickers, and watch her create a treasure chest of her own.

◀ *IF YOUR CHILD ENJOYS THIS ACTIVITY,* *also try Paint Primer, page 146.*

162

TURN AROUND

A SING-WHILE-YOU-SPIN SONG

THIS MOVE-YOUR-BODY SONG is a fun way to combine singing with some vigorous exercise. Sing "Turn Around" a few times, following the instructions in the lyrics, and exaggerate your actions—for example, leap high in the air when you sing, "Up we go!" Your little jumping bean will love imitating you; at the same time he'll develop better body control and gross motor skills. Acting out the lyrics also improves your child's comprehension of up and down and high and low.

MOVING TO THE MUSIC helps his body confidence grow by leaps and bounds.

to the tune of **"Frère Jacques"**

Perform the actions as indicated by the lyrics; do them slowly until your child understands all the movements.

**Turn around,
turn around,
touch your toes,
touch your toes.**

**Do a little jumping,
do a little jumping.**

Squat real low.

✔ **Balance**

✔ **Coordination**

✔ **Gross Motor Skills**

IF YOUR CHILD ENJOYS THIS ACTIVITY, also try Head to Toes, page 112.

MINI MIMES

ACTING OUT A TEA PARTY

SHE WANTS TO DO just about everything you do, right? Let her participate in grown-up activities by miming all sorts of fun things along with you.

• Try having a tea party—with no tea set. Act out pouring the tea, passing the plate of biscuits, and drinking and eating. Be sure to say "Please," "Thank you," and "Mmm . . . this is delicious!" That helps her to learn good manners, and it brings the party to life.

• Next: bake a cake together without any pans or ingredients. Crack the pretend eggs, mix in the flour, and pour the batter into a pan. Don't forget to dust the flour off your hands when you're all done— and then treat your-selves to a big piece of scrumptious cake.

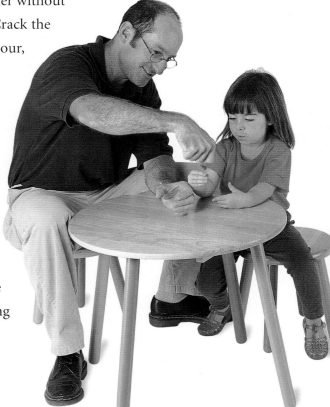

• Other activities to act out include flying an aeroplane, cleaning up the house, or perhaps galloping around on a horse.

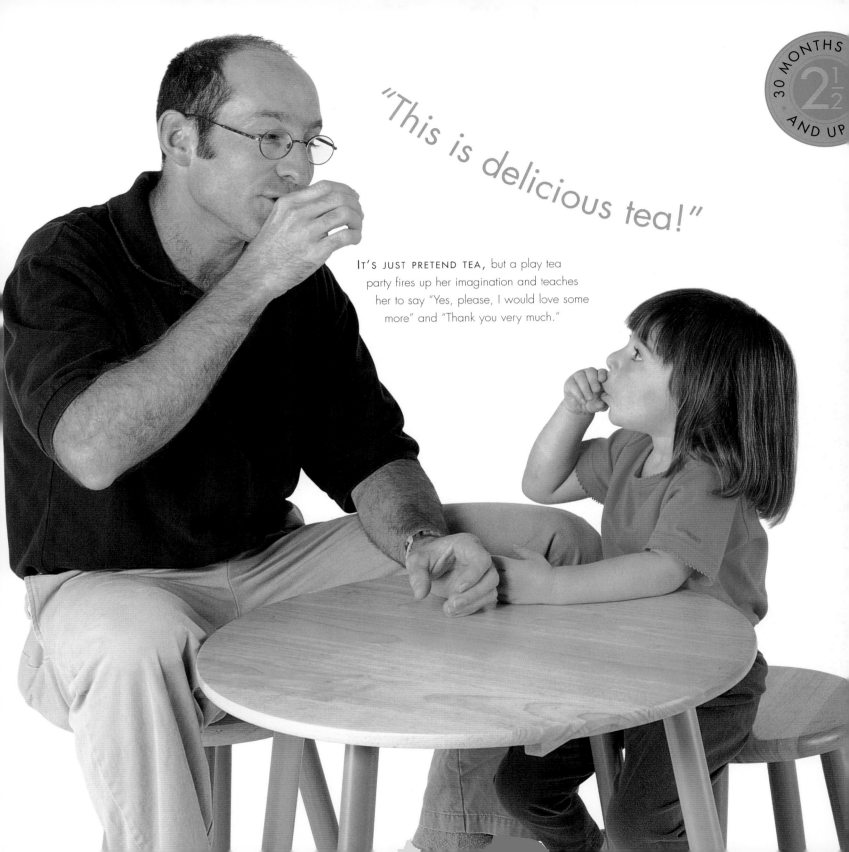

"This is delicious tea!"

IT'S JUST PRETEND TEA, but a play tea party fires up her imagination and teaches her to say "Yes, please, I would love some more" and "Thank you very much."

30 MONTHS
2½
AND UP

CAR CAPERS

A MATCHING-COLOURS GAME

SKILLSPOTLIGHT

Successfully matching colours *helps train a toddler's eye to compare and contrast different objects. It also engages his mind by making him link up two very different items that share one common characteristic (in this case, colour). And repeating the names of the colours aloud as he matches the car to the paper helps strengthen his vocabulary.*

Classifying Skills	✔
Concept Development	✔
Problem Solving	✔
Visual Discrimination	✔

IF YOUR CHILD ENJOYS THIS ACTIVITY, also try Shape Sorter, page 175. ▶

MOST TWO-YEAR-OLDS are fascinated by colours and are compelled to identify them. This activity takes advantage of your child's interest in colours while strengthening his ability to recognize them. Just find some paper that matches the colours of the cars or lorries and other vehicles in his toy collection. Call out the colour of the paper as you lay it on the floor. Park a car of the same colour on each piece of paper (red car on red paper, yellow lorry on yellow paper, for example). Then mix them up and ask your child to "drive" the vehicles onto their correct, colour-coded parking spots.

FINDING THE RIGHT parking place helps him begin to recognize what two different objects have in common.

FUNNY FACES

TALKING ABOUT FEELINGS

YOUR TODDLER is just beginning to understand the concept of emotions—that he feels happy sometimes and perhaps angry or sad at other times. Wooden spoon puppets can help him identify and express his feelings in appropriate ways. Draw a happy face, a sad face, and an angry face on three wooden spoons. You can also dress them up with coloured paper: add hair, a moustache, or a bow tie. Have the spoons express their "feelings" to your child or to each other. The happy-face spoon can say, "Oh boy! I'm going to the zoo today!" And the angry face can say, "No! I don't want to wear my coat!" Encourage your child to express his emotions, too.

SKILLSPOTLIGHT

Up until a few months ago, *your child probably had only one way of expressing "difficult" feelings: crying. Now he's getting old enough to say when he's happy, sad, or angry. Spoon puppets can model such conversations for him. Notice how he's getting rather demanding these days? Let the happy-face spoon show him how to politely ask for a glass of water instead of insisting on one.*

✔	**Concept Development**
✔	**Creative Expression**
✔	**Language Development**
✔	**Social Skills**

IT'S OFTEN EASIER for children to express themselves through play—so let your toddler practise talking about feelings with spoon puppets.

TODDLER TALK

JUST AS CHILDREN seem to come into this world hard-wired to learn language, parents instinctively do much to promote this vital skill. For one thing, throughout countless cultures around the world, they naturally speak to their babies and toddlers in a high-pitched, repetitive, singsong voice that linguists have dubbed "parentese." It is now universally accepted that this melodic, pared-down speech speeds up a child's ability to connect words with the objects they represent and offers the simplified syntax and repetition she needs to learn many of the rules of grammar.

Parents can do several other things to help. As the Research Report on page 59 highlights, the simple act of talking to your child—a lot—even before she is capable of talking back is critical to building her vocabulary. "Tell your baby and toddler everything you can think of," advise Dr. Marian Diamond and Janet Hopson in *Magic Trees of the Mind*. "Bathe your child with spoken language." Having a toddler point to the pictures in a book, echo some of your words, or add sound effects keeps her engaged and helps stretch her attention span.

Introducing new words in a real-life, emotional context also is important—a child picks up the meaning of "later" and "now" much more quickly when the words are linked to the time that she's going to get a favourite snack or go to the park. Feeding her boundless interest in knowing the names of everything she sees in the house, passes in the car, or spots in the local market is key to fulfilling her labelling instinct, which is going full throttle as she approaches her second birthday. Finally, don't forget the benefits of hands-on parenting: cuddling a child as you talk or read together adds a dimension of loving, physical contact that also seems to hasten language acquisition. ■

MIGHTY MEGAPHONES

30 MONTHS AND UP

2½

FUN WITH BOOMING VOICES

SHE'S SPEAKING quite well now, and her vocalizations often range from a murmur (when she's "reading" to her teddy bear) to a shriek (when it's time to leave the playground). You can expand her verbal and auditory skills even further with a paper megaphone. Just roll up a big sheet of thick paper and show her how talking into the small end of the cone can change the tone, direction, and volume of her voice. Take turns talking loudly and softly with the megaphone—or use it for amplifying songs and silly sounds.

SKILL SPOTLIGHT

Children naturally explore *their senses during play, but this activity encourages a focused exploration of listening and making sounds. Toddlers are also natural performers (hence the physical frenzy that often greets guests). Improvising with this makeshift device helps turn up the volume on their creativity.*

✔	**Cause & Effect**
✔	**Creative Expression**
✔	**Listening Skills**
✔	**Sensory Exploration**

NOW HEAR THIS: She'll love expanding her vocal range with this improvised amplifier.

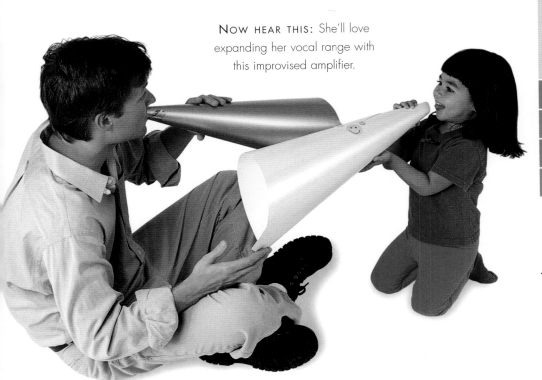

IF YOUR CHILD ENJOYS THIS ACTIVITY, also try Animal Actors, page 180. ▶

169

RIBBON RINGS

FANCY DANCING WITH FLYING STREAMERS

SKILL SPOTLIGHT

When you add *ribbon rings to a toddler's dance session, she'll become more aware of how she's moving her arms and body to make the ribbons float in different ways. This helps her develop gross motor skills and coordination. The rings also encourage rhythm exploration as well as creativity.*

Body Awareness	✔
Coordination	✔
Creative Movement	✔
Gross Motor Skills	✔
Rhythm Exploration	✔

SHE ALREADY LOVES to dance, but adding rings of colourful, floating ribbon will make her spinning and twirling all the more magical—and fun.

- Purchase a pair of ribbon rings (sold at specialty toy shops) or make your own by buying a dozen fabric ribbons or cutting fabric or old sheets into strips that are between 30 and 64 cm (12 and 25 inches) in length. Securely tie one end of each of the ribbons or strips around small embroidery rings or plastic bangles.

170

30 MONTHS
2½
AND UP

• Talk to your child about the different colours of the ribbons and ask her to show you which one is her favourite.

• Show her how to incorporate the rings into her dance routine: wave them up and down and swing them from side to side.

• Play dancing music you both enjoy and join your toddler as she swings to the beat and makes the ribbons float and twirl.

• Put the rings on the floor and dance around them, or pass the rings back and forth as you sashay past each other. Encourage her to improvise with her pretty new props.

CHILDREN LOVE THE COLOUR, motion, and drama of these rippling ribbons as they spin and dance across the room.

IF YOUR CHILD ENJOYS THIS ACTIVITY, also try Scarf Tricks, page 118.

171

MAGNIFY MATTERS

SKILL SPOTLIGHT

Using a magnifying glass *is a superb way to help a child appreciate nature. When a leaf isn't just a leaf but a complex maze of intersecting lines, or when a tiny insect suddenly has eyes, legs, and a mouth, your toddler learns that nature is rich and complex. Helping her describe what she sees builds her vocabulary, too.*

Concept Development	✔
Language Development	✔
Size & Shape Discrimination	✔
Tactile Stimulation	✔
Visual Discrimination	✔

ENHANCE YOUR CHILD'S curiosity about her world—and her understanding of it—with a magnifying glass. She'll marvel at how grains of sand look like multi-coloured boulders and how flat green leaves are etched with tiny lines.

• Start your exploration by taking your child on a walk outdoors. Show her how to hold the magnifying glass up to different objects—such as leaves, rocks, grass, flowers, sand, even insects—and look through it. Encourage her to touch the objects under scrutiny and help her find the appropriate words to describe them.

• Talk about concepts of size ("That pebble was little until we looked at it with the magnifying glass. Now it looks really big!"). Be sure to

AN ORDINARY ROCK and pinecone become intriguing landscapes of texture when your child has the chance to examine them up close and personal.

exercise extreme caution on sunny days; when the sun's rays are shining through the magnifying glass they can burn skin or even start a fire.

● Take her for a walk indoors, too. Tell her to get an up-close view of a blanket, her toast, a houseplant, her stuffed animals, or the hair on your pet. Ask her to describe what she sees, suggesting words if she doesn't have the vocabulary.

● Also use the magnifying glass to build body awareness. Let her explore her toes, fingerprints—and even your eyes and tongue.

30 MONTHS
2½
AND UP

RAIN-STICK MUSIC

EXPLORING NATURAL SOUNDS

SKILLSPOTLIGHT

Back when your toddler *was a baby, a rattle was a curious toy he loved to grasp with his little fingers. Now he can experience a large "rain" rattle, which will enhance his auditory perception as he learns to listen to it and compare the sound it makes with the sound of real rain.*

Creative Movement	✔
Listening Skills	✔
Sensory Exploration	✔

◀ *IF YOUR CHILD ENJOYS THIS ACTIVITY, also try Mystery Sounds, page 141.*

THE LOOK AND SOUND of rain fascinates most toddlers—it's water that mysteriously pours down from the sky, after all. You can re-create the sound of rain anytime with a "rain stick." Buy wooden ones at museum gift shops, or colourful plastic rain sticks at toy shops. You can also make your own by filling a poster tube with a cup of rice and securely capping both ends. Encourage your child to slowly turn his rain stick upside down while you're reading stories or singing about the rain. On stormy days, ask your toddler to listen to the real rain— then encourage him to listen to the similar sounds he can make with his special stick.

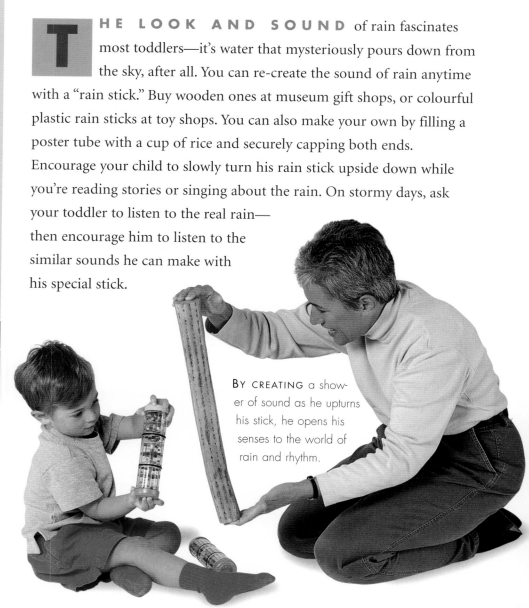

BY CREATING a shower of sound as he upturns his stick, he opens his senses to the world of rain and rhythm.

SHAPE SORTER

IDENTIFYING AND CLASSIFYING SHAPES

HERE'S A QUICK AND EASY activity that helps your child learn to organize different shapes. Simply collect an assortment of small balls and square-shaped blocks and mix them up in a pile. Put out a large bowl and a big box. Ask your child to place all of the round balls in the round bowl and the blocks in the box. It may take a few tries, but with your help he'll soon be sorting the shapes with ease.

PUTTING ROUND OBJECTS and square-shaped blocks into larger, similarly shaped containers helps him sort out the differences among shapes and sizes.

SKILLSPOTLIGHT

This classifying game *strengthens fundamental skills: identifying and organizing objects by a distinguishing characteristic—in this case, shape. Your toddler will also begin to understand that shapes come in many different sizes (that is, a ball is round and a bowl is round, but the bowl is a larger round-shaped object).*

✔	**Classifying Skills**
✔	**Concept Development**
✔	**Size & Shape Dixcrimination**

IF YOUR CHILD ENJOYS THIS ACTIVITY, also try Leaf Lineup, page 177. ▶

COUNT AND SEEK

FINDING THE MATCHING OBJECTS

SKILLSPOTLIGHT

Finding the objects *will boost your child's self-esteem (so don't hide the objects too well). Counting aloud as he finds them will help him learn both the sequence of numbers and an elementary concept of addition. The challenge of finding an object that he saw just a few moments ago also helps build visual memory.*

Counting Concepts	✓
Visual Discrimination	✓
Visual Memory	✓

IF YOUR CHILD ENJOYS THIS ACTIVITY, also try Flashlight Fun, page 148.

YOUNG CHILDREN of all ages love finding a hidden object—whether it's a baby's rattle, Mummy's face, or a biscuit hidden in Daddy's pocket. Asking a child to find more than one object adds counting practice to the fun. Simply collect three or more similar items such as cups, shoes, wooden spoons, or coloured balls. Show them to your toddler, hide them around the house (be sure to leave a part of the "hidden" objects exposed so your child can find them more readily), then ask him to search for them. Count out loud and applaud every time he finds one. To make the game harder, hide more matching objects.

LOOKING FOR "ONE MORE" introduces the concept of numbers into the treasure hunt.

176

LEAF LINEUP

SORTING BY SIZE

YOUR CHILD IS QUITE INTENT on identifying his possessions ("That's my spoon!") and sorting them into various categories ("These are my hats. These are my shoes."). Take advantage of his dual love of possessions and sorting by creating a leaf collection. Gather small, medium, and large leaves. Tape one example of each size onto the sides of paper bags or small boxes. Place the rest of the leaves in a pile. Ask your child to sort the leaves into the correct bag or box according to size. While he sorts, talk to him about the leaves—where they came from, for instance, and their colours. Having a hard time finding leaves? Cut out some leaf shapes from coloured paper.

SKILL SPOTLIGHT

Categorizing things *is immensely interesting for toddlers because it's a way of organizing and even controlling the world around them. This activity lets them learn the concepts of big and small and practise identifying which objects are which size. Talking about leaves also teaches children the words for colours and sizes and gives them a brief nature lesson.*

✔	Classifying Skills
✔	Concept Development
✔	Language Development
✔	Size & Shape Discrimination

WHAT GOES WHERE? Sorting a leaf collection is a great way to expand his understanding of big, medium, and small.

177

DUST BUSTING IS a job toddlers adore so let your little helper make this task more fun for you—and let her know that her work is appreciated.

RESEARCH REPORT

Many parents are surprised at the gusto a young child will bring to everyday activities such as sweeping the floor or sponging off a counter. Yet almost a century ago, an Italian physician and educator named Maria Montessori trumpeted the value of meaningful jobs—among many other revolutionary notions about early childhood. She said such chores help promote a child's sense of responsibility and self-esteem, and allow her to feel like she's contributing to the family or classroom. Today at the thousands of schools worldwide where teaching is based on Montessori's theories, classrooms are stocked with low-standing sinks, pint-size brooms and mops, and other cleaning supplies, and even the youngest preschoolers are expected to help.

COPYCAT

IMITATING THE ADULT WORLD

SHE'S CARRYING YOUR HANDBAG and talking to the pets the same way you do. Sometimes it's delightful and sometimes it's embarrassing: do you really say, "Get down!" in that tone of voice? Now make imitation a joint activity—and get some jobs done in the process.

- Encourage your child to "help" you rake leaves, dust, sweep, build a birdhouse, or fix a broken step. You can give her tot-size tools or safe adult ones, or just let her perform her tasks with make-believe supplies. She'll love giving you a helping hand.

- If you have a family pet, ask your toddler to help you feed, groom, exercise, or play with it. Not only will she learn new skills, she'll also learn to nurture the animal just as you nurture her.

- A garden is an ideal place for a child to lend a hand. Demonstrate how to plant seeds, then let her try. When the planting is long forgotten and the first shoots come up, you can surprise your young gardener by showing her the fruits of her labour.

- Adding music to your projects is a great way to enhance any task—especially if you whistle (or sing) while you work.

IF YOUR CHILD ENJOYS THIS ACTIVITY, also try Mini Mimes, page 164.

SKILL SPOTLIGHT

Children learn *by observing others —especially their parents. This wonderfully interactive activity is a good way to show your child day-to-day chores (although she's not ready to be assigned large tasks yet). It also boosts her confidence as she pretends to accomplish what Mummy and Daddy do. Imitating your voice and gestures builds auditory and visual skills; doing it to music helps her explore rhythm.*

✔	**Coordination**
✔	**Gross Motor Skills**
✔	**Listening Skills**
✔	**Role-Playing**
✔	**Social Skills**

179

ANIMAL ACTORS

IMITATING THE ANIMAL WORLD

SKILL SPOTLIGHT

It takes balance, *strength, and even coordination to stalk like a lion, to sweep a "trunk" along the ground, or to mimic a bird flying above the treetops. Pretending to be an animal also gives wings to your child's imagination and helps her develop empathy for other creatures in the world.*

Concept Development	✔
Creative Movement	✔
Gross Motor Skills	✔
Imagination	✔

SHE BARKS at the dog and crawls alongside the cat, and seeing the animals at the zoo makes her mad with excitement. Toddlers adore animals and the funny ways they move and "speak." Help your child explore the beauty of beasts by teaching her how to mimic other animals as well.

• Begin by looking at animal pictures in books and magazines with your toddler and talking about their behaviour—how they walk, what they eat, where they live, and the ways they communicate. Also assemble her stuffed animals and explain what life would be like for them if they were real creatures that didn't live propped up against her pillow.

YOUR LITTLE MONKEY enhances her imagination and physical agility as she apes the animals she sees.

30 MONTHS
2½
AND UP

- Demonstrate the sounds each animal makes: the bear growls, the cat meows, the rooster crows, and the frog croaks. Then ask your child to roar, purr, or "ribbit" like the animals she sees at the park or in cartoons, videos, or at the zoo.

- Also show her the actions of various animals: a duck waddles, a horse trots, a frog hops from lily pad to lily pad, a monkey swings from branch to branch, and an elephant uses its trunk to pull leaves from the trees. Ask her to waddle, trot, jump, swing her arms, and stretch the same way the animals do.

IF YOUR CHILD ENJOYS THIS ACTIVITY, also try Mini Mimes, page 164.

GLOSSARY

A

ABSTRACT THOUGHT
The ability to imagine and discuss people, ideas, and objects when they are not physically present. Pretending, notions of time, finding a lost object, and making plans to visit a friend all require some degree of abstract thought.

AUDITORY DEVELOPMENT
The maturation of a child's auditory system, which is necessary for spoken language development.

B

BALANCE
The ability to assume and maintain body positions against the force of gravity. A sense of balance is crucial for learning how to sit, stand, walk, run, jump, skate, and ride a bike.

BILATERAL COORDINATION
The ability to use both sides of the body simultaneously, whether or not the movements are symmetrical. A child needs bilateral coordination to crawl, walk, swim, climb, catch, and jump.

BODY AWARENESS
An understanding of what limbs, joints, and muscles feel like and the ability to locate one's body parts.

C

CAUSE & EFFECT
How one action affects another. Experience with cause and effect helps a child learn how her actions create a result ("When you drop the toy truck from the high chair, it falls on the floor.").

CLASSIFYING SKILLS
The ability to group objects according to a common characteristic, such as size, shape, or colour.

COGNITION
Mental or intellectual abilities, including recognizing, classifying, and comparing objects; remembering routines, people, and object placement; making judgments; and problem solving.

CONCEPT AWARENESS
An understanding of specific concepts, such as open/closed and big/little, gained through play, exploration, movement, and experience.

COORDINATION
The ability to integrate all of the senses to produce a movement response that is smooth, efficient, and skillful, such as kicking a ball.

COUNTING CONCEPTS
The ability to recite numbers in the correct order and to recognize one-to-one correspondence.

CREATIVE EXPRESSION
Using voice, movement, or art (such as painting or drawing) to communicate feelings and ideas.

CREATIVE MOVEMENT
Using bodily motion to communicate feelings and ideas.

D

DENDRITES
Branching nerve cells that carry nerve impulses within the brain. Researchers believe mental stimulation increases the size and complexity of dendrite networks, which in turn improves a child's cognition.

E

EYE-FOOT COORDINATION

Gauging distance and depth with the eyes and processing that information to coordinate when and where to place the feet. Eye-foot coordination is required, for example, when kicking a ball, running up steps, and walking on an uneven path.

EYE-HAND COORDINATION

Directing the position and motion of the hands (when catching a ball, for instance) in response to visual information.

F

FINE MOTOR SKILLS

Control of the small muscles, especially those in the hands, to execute small movements, such as picking up a raisin, cutting with scissors, writing, and using buttons, poppers, and shoelaces.

G

GROSS MOTOR SKILLS

Control of the large muscles, such as those in the arms and legs. Gross motor activities include walking, running, and climbing.

I

IMAGINATION

The ability to form mental images of what is not present. Imagination involves the act of creating new ideas by combining past experiences. It also involves abstract thought and enables a child to practise roles, predict outcomes of his behaviour, and create new scenarios.

L

LANGUAGE DEVELOPMENT

The complex process of acquiring language skills including understanding human speech, producing sounds and spoken language, and learning how to read and write.

GLOSSARY

LISTENING SKILLS

The ability to discern various sounds, including music, rhythm, pitch, and the intonation of spoken language.

LOGICAL REASONING

The ability to make decisions or take actions based on an understood progression of facts or physical characteristics. Sorting, nesting, and stacking objects all depend on logical reasoning, as does a toddler's understanding that she needs to drag a chair over to her father's desk in order to reach his computer.

N

NEURONS

Long nerve cells that carry electrical impulses throughout the body. Different kinds of nerve cells enable us to move our body, think, use our senses, and experience emotions.

P

PROBLEM SOLVING

The ability to work out a solution to a mental or physical puzzle. A toddler solves a problem when he figures out how to screw a lid on a jar or pick up his cup without letting go of his stuffed animal.

R

REFLEXES

Automatic responses to stimuli and events (such as putting your hand up to stop a ball from hitting you).

RHYTHM EXPLORATION

The act of exploring the rhythms and underlying beat of music through movement.

ROLE-PLAYING

Using the imagination to pretend that you are someone or something else. Role-playing helps a child explore her feelings.

S

SELF-CONCEPT

A child's understanding that he is an individual person. A child with a good self-concept feels good about himself.

SENSORY EXPLORATION

Using the senses of touch, hearing, sight, smell, and taste to learn about the world.

SHAPE RECOGNITION

The ability to identify specific forms, such as circles and triangles. Shape recognition eventually helps a child learn to read and write.

SIZE & SHAPE DISCRIMINATION

The ability to identify objects of different dimensions and their relationship to each other, such as "the big dog," "the little kitty," and "the square box."

SOCIAL SKILLS

Interacting and relating appropriately to other people, including sharing and taking turns and recognizing other people's emotions.

SPATIAL AWARENESS

Knowing where one's own body is in relation to other people and objects. A child uses spatial awareness to crawl under a bed, walk through doorways, and generally move through space.

SYNAPSES

The tiny gaps between neurons through which electrical impulses jump, thus allowing nerve cells to communicate with one another.

T

TACTILE DISCRIMINATION

The ability to determine differences in shape or texture by touch. Being able to discern textures helps children explore and understand their environment and recognize objects ("I have a soft feather and a cold stone in my pocket.").

TACTILE STIMULATION

Input to receptors that respond to pressure, temperature, pain, and the movement of hairs on the skin. Tactile stimulation enables a child to feel comfortable with new experiences such as first foods and unexpected touch.

U

UPPER BODY STRENGTH

The development of muscles in the neck, shoulders, arms, and upper trunk. Such development is crucial to crawling, pulling up, and carrying heavy objects.

V

VISUAL DISCRIMINATION

The ability to focus on and distinguish objects within a visual field. A toddler uses visual discrimination to find a bird in a picture or locate a parent in a crowd of people.

VISUAL MEMORY

The ability to recall objects, faces, and images. Visual memory allows a child to remember a sequence of objects or pictures and is a foundation for learning to read.

185

SKILLS INDEX

187

SKILLS INDEX

INDEX

ACKNOWLEDGMENTS

A VERY SPECIAL THANKS to all the toddlers, parents, and grandparents featured in this book:

Robin & Jessica Alvarado
Eric Anderson
José & Anna Arcellana
Lisa & Summer Atwood
Debbie & Karly Baker
Madeleine Barnum
Leticia & Mikailah Bassard
Dana & Nicholas Bisconti
Annamaria & Sean Mireles
 Boulton
Catherine & Lizzie Boyle
Jackson Breuner-Brooks
Ashley Bryant
Madison Carbone
Christian Chubbs
Jamila Coleman
Kevin & Sofia Colosimo
Kim & Katherine Daifotis
Jane & Robert Davis
Keeson Davis
Kimberly & Jacob Dreyer
Margaret & Lauren Dunlap
Stacy, Sydney, & Sophie
 Dunne
Tiffany & Simon Eng
Edgar & Melanie Estonina
Christina Fallone
Kristen & Kaitlin Fenn &
 Susan Carlson
Terri & Jacob Giamartino

Sharon & Annabel
 Gonzalez
Carrie Green-Zinn &
 Zaria Zinn
Jade & Jordan Greene
Annette, Katie, & Connor
 Hagan
Drew Harris
Arthur & Reed Haubenstock
Cameron & Bix Hirigoyen
Laurasia Holzman-Smith
Rochelle Jackson
Ryan Jahabli-Danekas
David Johnson
Lynne Jowett & Eloise Shaw
Elana Kalish
Gilda & Megan Kan
Caecilia Kim & Addison
 Brenneman
Olivier & Raphael Laude
Mark & Samantha Leeper
Mary & Simon Lindsay
Darien & Nicholas Lum
Peg Mallery & Elliot Dean
Ryan McCarty
Susan McKeever & Sophia
 Rosney
Alex Mellin
Justin Miloslavich
Lou, Terri, & Lou Molinaro

Tom, Genevieve, & Graham
 Morgan
Madeleine Myall
Betsy & Megumi Nakamura
Abby Newbold
Carly Olson
Terry, Kim, & Hunter
 Patterson
Elizabeth & Hayden Payne
Henrietta & Katie Plessas
Jim & Kira Pusch
Shanti Rachlis
Wayne & Thomas Riley
Kali Roberts
Blake Rotter
Leigh & Kai Sata
Haley Shipway
Kathryn Siegler
David Sparks
Jackie & Jaylyn Stemple
Brisa & Diva Stevens
Eloisa Tejero & Isabella Shin
Alisa & David Tomlinson
Lila & April Torres
Mahsati & Kiana Tsao
Paula Venables
Sebastian & Julian von Nagel
Gabriel Wanderley
Jenifer Warren & Grace
 Bailey

Pernille & Sebastian
 Wilkenschildt
Daisy & Karinna Wong
Sara Wong & Dean
 & Jack Fukushima
Tina & Anna Wood
Amy & Marissa Wright
Jill & Nicole Zanolli
Lisa Zuniga & Maria
 Carlsen

*Mirror on page 60 courtesy of
Mudpie in San Francisco. Crayola
and serpentine design are registered
trademarks of Binney & Smith and
are used with permission.*